Green Finance and Investment

Clean Energy Finance and Investment Roadmap of the Philippines

OECD

BETTER POLICIES FOR BETTER LIVES

Please cite this publication as:
OECD (2024), *Clean Energy Finance and Investment Roadmap of the Philippines*, Green Finance and Investment, OECD Publishing, Paris, https://doi.org/10.1787/7a13719d-en.

ISBN 978-92-64-97742-6 (print)
ISBN 978-92-64-56763-4 (PDF)
ISBN 978-92-64-71015-3 (HTML)
ISBN 978-92-64-94080-2 (epub)

Green Finance and Investment
ISSN 2409-0336 (print)
ISSN 2409-0344 (online)

Revised version, April 2024
Details of revisions available at: https://www.oecd.org/about/publishing/Corrigendum_Clean_Energy_Finance_and_Investment_Roadmap_of_the_Philippines.pdf

Photo credits: Cover © umikem/Shutterstock.com.

Corrigenda to OECD publications may be found on line at: www.oecd.org/about/publishing/corrigenda.htm.

Preface

The Philippines has stepped up its efforts to reduce carbon dioxide emissions in recent years: The country submitted its first Nationally Determined Contribution (NDC) in April 2021, committing to a 75% emission reduction during the period 2020 – 2030, against a business-as-usual scenario. To achieve these emissions reductions, the country's National Renewable Energy Program 2020-2040 aims to more than double the electricity generated by renewable sources in its power mix by 2040 compared to today's levels, while reducing its economy-wide energy intensity by 3% over the same period.

Achieving these targets will require unlocking USD 337 billion in cumulative investments to 2040. The *OECD Clean Energy Finance and Investment Mobilisation (CEFIM)* programme aims to strengthen domestic enabling conditions to attract finance and investments in renewables, energy efficiency and decarbonisation of industry in emerging economies. This *Clean Energy Finance and Investment Roadmap of the Philippines* ("the Roadmap") provides tailored recommendations for the Government of the Philippines to help unlock finance and investment in clean energy. The analyses also bring international experiences from other countries that can serve as examples for similar measures tailored to the Philippines' national circumstances.

The Roadmap focuses on two clean energy sectors that were identified and selected in consultation with the Department of Energy (DOE) of the Government of the Philippines: offshore wind power, and energy efficiency in the building sector, with a focus on public buildings. Offshore wind, with its vast untapped potential along the over 17 thousand kilometres of Philippine coastline, stands out as an opportunity to decarbonise the country's power sector, with the potential to supply 23% of the country's electricity by 2050. Promoting the benefits of energy efficiency in public buildings could help reduce energy consumption in the building sector, which is one of the largest consumers of electricity in the Philippines, and help institutionalise and promote energy efficiency and conservation across all sectors in the country.

Supporting the energy transition and the development of the energy efficiency market can also deliver strong economic benefits for the Philippines, including through raising economic growth, increased domestic tax revenues, and the restructuring and development of rural and coastal communities. It provides opportunities for human capacity development and the creation of long-term and highly skilled jobs, including through retraining the local workforce for careers across the green energy supply chain and incentivising skills transfers from the oil and gas sector.

The insights and recommendations presented in this Roadmap will help the Philippines strengthen conditions to attract the much-needed investments for the country's clean energy transition. Going forward, the OECD can support the Government of the Philippines in implementing the Roadmap's recommendations, including through tailored capacity building and knowledge sharing activities, to boost investments in offshore wind and energy efficiency.

Mathias Cormann
Secretary-General, OECD

Foreword

The Clean Energy Finance and Investment Roadmap of the Philippines ("the Roadmap") and supporting analysis presented in this report aim to help the Philippines align its clean energy ambition with economic growth. Since the Government of the Philippines gives a prominent role to offshore wind deployment and accelerated energy efficiency improvements to ensure a sustainable, affordable and resilient energy system, while supporting the country's economic development and environmental objectives, the topics of offshore wind and energy efficiency in public buildings were selected for this Roadmap as key focus areas in the near term to put the country on a path to decarbonisation.

The Roadmap was developed by the Organisation for Economic Co-operation and Development (OECD) Clean Energy Finance and Investment Mobilisation (CEFIM) Programme in close co-operation with the Government of the Philippines, including the Department of Energy (DOE). It also brought together the public and private sectors to agree upon a clear action plan that identifies and addresses bottlenecks complicating or constraining finance and investment in the Philippines' clean energy sector, thereby contributing to operationalise the country's energy plans. It also complements the financial sector priorities to promote sustainable practices through corporate social responsibility and business responsibility reporting.

The process for drafting the Roadmap included workshops with experts and key stakeholders to identify barriers and develop possible solutions.[1] Thanks to the fruitful discussions in these workshops, key financing solutions were identified, roadmap findings were discussed, and consensus was reached on the roadmap actions and areas of recommendation. These have also been supported with data and analysis from other studies and research.

The first section of this report presents a draft roadmap action plan for the Government of the Philippines to consider in order to mobilise finance and investment in offshore wind power and energy efficiency in public buildings. The following sections present supporting analysis: Chapter 1 presents an overview of key trends and market developments for renewable energy and energy efficiency in the Philippines; Chapter 2 analyses the ways to mobilise finance and investments for offshore wind; and Chapter 3 presents emerging financial mechanisms and business models for energy efficiency in the public sector.

This report is an output of the OECD Environment Policy Committee (EPOC) and its new Working Party on Finance and Investment for Environmental Goals (WPFIEG). The Clean Energy Finance and Investment Roadmap of the Philippines is one of the key outputs of the OECD CEFIM Programme. The CEFIM Programme aims to support governments in selected emerging economies in South and Southeast Asia, Latin America and Africa to enable finance and investment in renewable electricity, energy efficiency and decarbonisation of industry ("clean energy"). The report was prepared with funding from the Government of Germany under the Sustainable Infrastructure Programme in Asia (SIPA).

The Roadmap was drafted and developed by Ariola Mbistrova, with inputs from Jeremy Faroi and Chetna Hareesh Kumar, under the supervision of Geraldine Ang, Team Lead for the OECD CEFIM Programme, as well as Krzysztof Michalak, Acting Head of the Finance, Investment and Global Relations (FIG) Division in the OECD Environment Directorate as well as Yuval Laster, new Head of the FIG Division. The authors are extremely grateful for the precious inputs and contribution from Assistant Secretary Mylene C. Capongcol, Director Michael O. Sinocruz, Director Patrick T. Aquino, Director Marissa P. Cerezo, Assistant Director Ruby B. de Guzman, Francis Richard O. Rabulan, Jane M. Peralta , Michael S. Leabres, Energy Policy and Planning Bureau - Planning Division (EPPB-PD), Energy Utilization Management Bureau (EUMB), and Renewable Energy Management Bureau (REMB) in the DOE. The authors are also very grateful for the valuable inputs from Cyril C. del Callar, Ricardo G. Barcelona, Carlos Miguel S. del Callar, and Gina Lourdes D. Valeros (Del Callar & Partners Co.).

The report has benefited from inputs from the following OECD and International Energy Agency (IEA) colleagues: Joseph Cordonnier, Batih Hakimul, Deger Saygin, Virginie Marchal (OECD), Cecilia Tam, Cornelia Schenk, Natalie Kauf (IEA). The report has also benefited from external reviews from: Quynh Chi Tri, Andrew Ho (Ørsted), Jerome Guillet (Sustainable Energy Now), Diana G. Connet (Asian Development Bank), Hadrian Vivek, Kalyani Basu, Hazim Rosli (Carbon Trust), Zahra Janipour (Rabobank), Ann Margret Francisco and Mark Hutchinson (GWEC).

Additional thanks are due to industry experts from broad consultations: Assistant Director Artemio P. Habitan (DOE), Jayson G. Corpuz Energy Regulatory Commission (ERC), Anne Montelibano Philippine Independent Power Producers Association (PIPPA), Maria Ayuso Olmedo (World Bank), Michael Baylosis National Grid Corporation of the Philippines (NGCP), Theo Sunico (Triconti), Kevin Banister (Simply Blue), Jo Ann Eala Bank of the Philippine Islands (BPI), Reinier A. Ilige (BPI Capital), Juan Martin L. Syquia (ACEN), Jonas Millqvist (EKF), Deano Christian Echague, Department of Budget and Management (DBM), Alexander Ablaza (Climargy), Shri Abhishek Gupta (EESL), Pedro L. Lite Jr., Philippine National Oil Company-Renewables Corporation (PNOC-RC), Neil Adrian S. Cabiles Department of Finance (DOF), Arnold Onrubia (Albay Govt), Yoshiko De Villa (ETP), Reno Joseph Cantre (PPP Centre), Lizet Ramirez (WindEurope), Tom Harries (Nardac), Jerome Guillet (Sustainable Energy Now), Mark Hutchinson and Ann Margret Francisco (GWEC).

The authors thank Dominique Haleva (OECD) for administrative support and editorial assistance. The authors also thank JQ&Ros Communications for graphic design.

The Roadmap was developed under the guidance of a Steering Committee comprised of representatives from diverse ministries across the government of the Philippines and chaired by the Department of Energy (DOE). Steering Committee members included:

- Felix William B. Fuentebella, Undersecretary, Department of Energy.
- Roderick M. Planta, OIC Undersecretary, National Economic and Development Authority;
- Ceferino S. Rodolfo, Undersecretary, Board of Investments;
- Maria Edita Tan, Undersecretary, Department of Finance;
- Gilbert C. Gonzales, Assistant Secretary, Department of Environment and Natural Resources;
- Lyn I. Javier, Assistant Governor, Bangko Sentral ng Pilipinas;
- Rustico Noli D. Cruz, Vice President, Development Bank of the Philippines; and
- Kelvin Lester K. Lee, Commissioner, Securities and Exchange Commission.

In addition, two Technical Working Groups were formed under the Steering Committee on renewable energy and energy efficiency, thanks to coordination from the DOE. These working groups deliberated key issues for clean energy projects and provided valuable feedback throughout the Roadmap process. They were comprised of representatives from government, industry, financial institutions, and policy advisors (Table 1).

Table 1. Technical Working Group Members

Renewable Energy	Energy Efficiency
Renewable Energy Management Bureau (REMB)	Energy Utilization and Management Bureau
National Economic and Development Authority (NEDA)	National Economic and Development Authority
Department of Finance (DOF)	Government Institutions
Department of Budget and Management (DBM)	Industry Associations, think tanks, and NGOs
Department of Environment and Natural Resources (DENR)	RE and EEC Project Developers
Energy Regulatory Commission (ERC)	Multilateral Development Partners
National Electrification Administration (NEA)	Donor Agencies (by Invitation)
National Transmission Corporation (TransCo)	Development Bank of the Philippines (DBP)
Board of Investments (BOI)	Land Bank of the Philippines (LBP)
Philippine Economic Zone Authority (PEZA)	Bank of the Philippine Islands (BPI)
Institute for Climate and Sustainable Cities (ICSC)	BDO Unibank, Inc.
United Nations Development Programme (UNDP)	
Philippine Independent Power Producers Association (PIPPA)	
National Renewable Energy Board (NREB)	
Development Bank of the Philippines (DBP)	
BDO Unibank, Inc.	
Land Bank of the Philippines (LBP)	
Philippine Guarantee Corporation (PGC)	
Independent Electricity Market Operator of the Philippines (IEMOP)	

This Roadmap was made possible through the generous contribution of Germany.

Table of contents

Tables

Figures

Boxes

Follow OECD Publications on:

https://twitter.com/OECD

https://www.facebook.com/theOECD

https://www.linkedin.com/company/organisation-eco-cooperation-development-organisation-cooperation-developpement-eco/

https://www.youtube.com/user/OECDiLibrary

https://www.oecd.org/newsletters/

This book has...

StatLinks

A service that delivers Excel® files from the printed page!

Look for the *StatLink* at the bottom of the tables or graphs in this book. To download the matching Excel® spreadsheet, just type the link into your Internet browser or click on the link from the digital version.

Abbreviations and units of measure

BOI	Board of Investments
CREATE	Corporate Recovery and Tax Incentives for Enterprises
CBI	Climate Bonds Initiative
CGIF	Credit Guarantee and Investment Facility
CREZ	Competitive Renewable Energy Zone
CSP	Competitive Selection Process
COD	Commissioning date
DENR	Department of Environment and Natural Resources
DOE	Department of Energy
DOST	Department of Science and Technology
ECA	Export Credit Agencies
EE&C	Energy Efficiency & Conservation
EESL	Energy Efficiency Services Limited
ETM	Energy Transition Mechanism
EVOSS	Energy Virtual One-Stop Shop
ERC	Energy Regulatory Commission
EPIRA	Electric Power Industry Reform Act
ESCO	Energy Services Company

ESI	Energy Savings Insurance
FDI	Foreign Direct Investment
FIP	Feed in Premium
FIT	Feed in Tariff
GCG	Governance Commission for Government-owned or Controlled Corporations
GEAR	Green Energy Auction Reserve
GEAP	Green Energy Auction Programme
GEMP	Government Energy Management Programme
GEOP	Green Energy Option Programme
GET	Green Energy Tariffs
IAEECC	Inter-Agency Energy Efficiency and Conservation Committee
IPP	Independent Power Producers
LCEP	Low Carbon Energy Programme
LiDAR	Light Detection and Ranging
LGU	Local Government Unit
LNG	Liquefied Natural Gas
LEECP	Local Energy Efficiency and Conservation Plan
NAMRIA	National Mapping and Resource Information Authority
NMP	Net Metering Programme
NPC	National Power Corporation
TransCo	National Transmission Corporation
NEDA	National Economic and Development Authority
NGCP	National Grid Corporation of the Philippines
NREP	National Renewable Energy Program
O&M	Operation and Maintenance

PDP	Power Development Plan
PEP	Philippine Energy Plan
PNOC-RC	Philippine National Oil Company – Renewables Corporation
POWJIP	Philippine Offshore Wind – Joint Industry Platform
PPA	Power Purchase Agreement
PPP	Public Private Partnership
PSA	Power Supply Agreement
RCOA	Retail Competition and Open Access
RPS	Renewable Portfolio Standards
TDP	Transmission Development Plan
WESM	Wholesale Electricity Spot Market
WESC	Wind Energy Service Contracts

Executive Summary

The Philippines is committed to reaching 50% renewable energy in the electricity mix by 2040, while achieving economy wide energy savings of 24% over the same period. Reaching these targets will require substantial efforts in the power sector and energy efficiency sector. The government recognises that the high investment required for this transformation would rely on the pooling of domestic and international resources from both public and private sectors. To this end, since 2022, the government has enacted regulation to remove foreign direct investment (FDI) restrictions in the energy sector.

This Clean Energy Finance and Investment Roadmap of the Philippines ("the Roadmap") outlines critical actions that the Government of the Philippines can consider to help unlock finance and investment in two clean energy sectors: (i) offshore wind; and (ii) energy efficiency in public buildings. The two sectors were identified and selected in consultation with the Philippines Department of Energy (DOE) to accelerate the country's decarbonisation pathways.

Offshore wind can play a key role in helping the country meet its national renewable energy targets. With over 17 thousand kilometres of coastline (Philippines Information Agency, 2023[1]), the Philippines is estimated to have a technical offshore wind potential of 178 GW, none tapped so far. Offshore wind for the Philippines also means less competition for land in a densely populated country (World Bank, 2022[2]). This Roadmap proposes a comprehensive set of measures that can improve the readiness of domestic markets in the Philippines to raise the capital needed to meet the country's offshore wind potential. Key priorities for attracting finance and boosting offshore wind investments in the Philippines include:

- Designing a regulatory framework that provides the right investment signals for investors and allows for projects to get built on time, cost effectively and with maximum local benefits.
- A planning and permitting process based on a one-stop shop approach that co-ordinates the involvement of over 20 agencies nationwide.
- Strategically planning for the necessary port and grid infrastructure to reliably support an emerging offshore wind market in the Philippines.
- Recognising the role of finance in supporting cost reduction pathways for offshore wind and fostering synergy and collaboration between international development finance and private finance.

Energy efficiency is another key pillar of the Philippines' strategy towards reaching its energy and climate targets. The energy efficiency market in the Philippines remains nascent and efforts are underway to promote the benefits of energy efficiency to help market scale-up. To this end, the government has adopted a strategy to lead by example and promote energy efficiency in public buildings. The Government Energy Management Program (GEMP) requires all government offices, including Local Government Units (LGUs), to reduce monthly electricity and petroleum products consumption by 10%, benchmarked against consumption averages in 2004 and 2005 (DOE, 2022[3]). To date, just under half of government entities are compliant. Key priorities for incentivising higher energy efficiency amongst LGUs include:

- Revising public procurement rules to accommodate energy efficiency projects with a payback period exceeding one year, including bundled projects that offer both product and service.

- Evaluating budgetary constraints of LGUs, the in-house technical knowledge and capacity that are needed to implement the National Energy Efficiency and Conservation Plan (NEECP) 2023 – 2050.
- Establishing a project pipeline for energy efficiency investments in the public sector via a designated aggregator entity to attract private equity investments.
- A focus on data collection and transparency that can improve the trust in the business model and improve access to funding from external non-government sources.

To maximise local content and benefit to the local communities, both offshore wind and energy efficiency sectors would need to rely on enhanced cross-government collaboration and integrated planning. Both sectors bring significant job creating potential in clean energy. As such, skills development and inclusivity are important contributors to local economic benefits. Capacity building, talent development and certification programmes for a well-trained workforce of technicians, engineers, financiers and service providers can help to accommodate a vibrant supply chain in the Philippines.

Roadmap Action Plan

This section provides an overview of a strategic framework to unlock finance and investment in offshore wind projects and energy efficiency in public buildings in the Philippines. This section serves as guidance for the central and local government in the Philippines, the private sector and the international development community active in the country, on attracting finance and boosting clean energy investments.

Enabling finance and investment in offshore wind power

Offshore wind can play a key role in helping the Philippines meet its renewable energy generation target of 35% by 2030 under the National Renewable Energy Plan (NREP) and 50% by 2040 (DOE, 2021[4]). With over 17 thousand kilometres of coastline, the Philippines is estimated to have a technical offshore wind potential of 178 GW. If fully harnessed, offshore wind has the potential to supply 23% of the country's electricity by 2050 (World Bank, 2022[2]). However, the country only has 0.7 GW of wind capacity installed to date, all of it onshore. Offshore wind for the Philippines offers opportunities to reframe how its marine resources are appropriately exploited to achieve its low carbon and development ambitions.

In a prior study, the World Bank set out a series of suggestions to develop the offshore wind market in the Philippines. This OECD report builds upon that work by providing a more granular view of the market and the steps needed to make offshore wind a viable option for the Philippines coastal regions. The recommendations below developed under this OECD Roadmap outline some key steps and actions that can ensure a rapid scale up of offshore wind in the Philippines, including:

- **Setting clear targets for fixed and floating offshore wind in power generation toward 2030 and beyond as a first step for development plans**. This should be underpinned by detailed provisions for licensing, permitting, grid connection and supply chain infrastructure such as ports, roads, manufacturing capacity. Ensuring a co-ordinated approach to maritime spatial planning, power development plans, national renewable energy plans, and transmission development plans is also essential. Enhanced cross-agency collaboration would allow the Government of the Philippines to convert the high offshore wind potential into bankable projects in addition to strengthening supply chain resilience and facilitate economies of scale.
- **Allocating development zones for fixed and floating offshore wind, to fast-track new projects, guide grid planning and improve procedures for transmission expansion.** By collecting geo-technical data for marine spatial planning, with the support of industry and development partners, the government can fully leverage economic potential of offshore wind. In doing so, this will also help identify appropriate areas for industrialisation through domestic supply chains, port upgrades and related infrastructure that will deliver co-benefits for local communities.
- **Integrating offshore wind into the country's Energy Virtual One-Stop Shop (EVOSS) and streamlining permitting procedures, to reduce administrative barriers and encourage new market entrants.** A clear configuration of roles and responsibilities for all the government agencies involved in offshore wind planning and permitting would allow for a successful roll-out of the

offshore wind EVOSS. Likewise, investing in digital tools, human resources and talent development for the offshore wind one-stop shop will ensure that the process is efficient and transparent.

- **Synchronising the buildout of offshore wind projects with the expansion of transmission infrastructure, to help mitigate risks such as grid congestion and power curtailment.** Accelerating the grid build out and optimising its use will be critical to deliver economically viable offshore wind projects in the Philippines by reducing potential risk premia and ensuring smooth system integration. This is highly dependent on the timely implementation of the centralised national grid project that interconnects the three main regions in the Philippines. In addition, streamlining project selection procedures for inclusion in the Transmission Development Plan (TDP) and ensuring close involvement of the DOE can help avoid connection delays. Proactive grid planning - jointly by the DOE and the National Grid Corporation of the Philippines (NGCP) - for larger volumes of offshore wind capacity additions, can lower the cost per project and investments needed for onshore grid upgrades.
- **Allocating offshore wind to a separate technology band in future rounds of Green Energy Auctions Programme (GEAP), to improve competition outcomes.** It is important to give to the industry visibility on timing, volumes and pricing. In parallel to the auctions, the government can also consider an open-door policy for a developer-led market, provided the planning and permitting for projects are secured.
- **Setting out revenue stabilisation measures at the early market stage will be important to attract low-cost and long-term finance for capital intensive offshore wind projects.** Early projects are important because they will help build the supply chain, a credible track record, and investor confidence, all of which can contribute to a lower cost of finance. In line with this, a transparent costing methodology needs to be developed for offshore wind prior to establish the ceiling prices – Green Energy Auction Reserve (GEAR) - in the current auction design. It is also important to continue with the inflation indexed tariff to mitigate macro-economic risks in a project.
- **Working with International Financial Institutions (IFIs) and Export Credit Agencies (ECAs) creates opportunities to unlock private capital for offshore wind development.** The roles and responsibilities of each of these institutions can rely on complementarity and collaboration. Regional Multilateral Development Banks (MDBs) can bridge the investment gap on the enabling infrastructure, port upgrades and other onshore support facilities. IFIs can set up first-loss guarantee financial instruments that can catalyse private sector investments. ECAs can intervene at project level to improve the risk absorption structure of a transaction.
- **Developing a skilled and well-trained workforce can improve the competitiveness of the offshore wind sector and advance efficient supply chains in the Philippines.** The government and international organisations can step up efforts to support development of human capital. This can include retraining the local Filipino workforce for careers in offshore wind across all the supply chain, incentives to transfer skills from the oil and gas sector or incentives to attract overseas Filipino professionals to bring their international experience from abroad.

Table 2. Offshore wind: key actions and recommendations

Key topic area	Actions [Timing: Short-term (S/T), Medium-term (M/T)]	Implementer
Long-term vision and common guiding principles	▪ Developing a comprehensive offshore wind strategy that considers industry risks and balances the country's energy transition with economic feasibility. [S/T] ▪ Setting specific and time-bound targets for offshore wind generation and installed capacity, with a clearly defined role for fixed-bottom and floating technologies. [S/T]	DOE, in collaboration with all agencies involved in offshore wind planning and permitting.
Enhanced cross-government collaboration	▪ Strengthening planning between agencies, central and local authorities, potentially through working groups for supply chain development and enabling infrastructure. [S/T] ▪ Integrating supply chain planning early on in industrial trade policies to facilitate the development of the required onshore supporting infrastructure. [S/T] ▪ Coordinating policy approaches across existing strategies such as Maritime Spatial Planning, Power Development Plans, National Renewable Energy Plans, and Transmission Development Plans. [M/T]	Cross-government, DOE, NGCP, TransCo, DENR, NAMRIA, DOTr, DOST, DOLE, International Development Partners
Data collection and resource assessment	▪ Allocating offshore wind development zones through data-driven decision making. This includes resource, spatial, bathymetric, geological, environmental, meteorological and socio-economic data. [S/T] ▪ Unifying and visualising all this information under a digital data room for investors, hosted under the DOE, and fully integrated in the offshore wind one-stop-shop to support project planning and permitting. [S/T] ▪ Collecting and adding other relevant data to the platform, including broader infrastructure planning such as suitable ports and transmission grids. Collaboration with wind energy developers during this process can ensure a focus on data that private investors are not well-positioned to collect. [M/T]	DOE, NAMRIA, International Development Partners
Offshore wind planning and permitting	▪ Revising guidelines for Wind Energy Service Contracts (WESC) to accommodate offshore wind specific activities, clarify any issues of tenurial rights and allocate realistic timelines to complete the pre-development activities. [S/T] ▪ Investing in digital tools and human resources helps streamline processes under the offshore wind one-stop shop and maintain open dialogue with industry. [S/T]	DOE, Government Agencies

Onshore support facilities and port upgrades	▪ Facilitating collaboration between port authorities and offshore wind energy developers to assess the readiness of priority ports. Establishing a baseline for required investments can feed into the business model, the financing structures, and any future infrastructure planning. [S/T] ▪ Considering a multi-port strategy, where different ports collaborate to provide different services during different stages of a project's lifecycle. This is particularly important for floating offshore wind, which has the highest technical potential in the Philippines. [S/T] ▪ Given their strategic nature, port related infrastructure can pool together a variety of investors. In the Philippines, the port assessment development phase is expected to be financed by the Asian Development Bank. Where needed, developers can also contribute to the initial port assessment phase and in the elaboration of the port development plans. [S/T] ▪ Securing crucial concessional finance from multilateral development banks in bridging some of the investment gap and complementing the existing short-term finance facilities of ports. [M/T] ▪ Improving investment certainty and a creating a bankable project pipeline to facilitate lending from commercial banks. Allocation of specific development zones, timely planning and permitting, and frontloaded auction schedule can provide investment certainty and showcase future utilization rates. [S/T]	Department of Energy (DOE) Department of Transportation (DOTr) The Philippines Port Authority (PPA) National Grid Corporation of the Philippines (NGCP) International Development Partners Wind energy developers Institutional investors; Multilateral development banks Commercial Banks
Grid networks and trans-mission planning	▪ Including offshore wind in the Competitive Renewable Energy Zones (CREZ) to match output with demand, in addition to facilitating some of the grid development, maritime spatial planning, ports capabilities and other supporting infrastructure. [S/T]	DOE, NGCP
	▪ Reforming and diversifying the project selection process for the transmission development plan and improving the efficiency of the current process of system impact studies, to allow a project to secure timely grid permit and connection. [S/T]	DOE, NGCP, ERC, International Development Partners
	▪ Clarifying asset boundary classifications under the grid code, to provide some transparency on the transmission line ownership and, when applicable, the recovery mechanism by TransCo. This can cover specific provisions throughout all stages of a project lifecycle, including decommissioning. [S/T]	DOE, NGCP, TransCo
Auction design and regulatory framework	▪ Using the country's Green Energy Auction Programme (GEAP) to enable industry development. The offshore wind auction model, including volumes and tariffs, will need to consider all the industry risks, actions and timelines mentioned above. [S/T] ▪ Creating a separate band under GEAP for offshore wind. Moreover, auction schedules can be frontloaded to provide investors across the entire supply chain with medium term visibility for financial and project planning. [S/T]	DOE, International Development Partners

	▪ Allowing early offshore wind projects to benefit from revenue stabilization based on transparent methodology for setting ceiling prices. This could be developed with established international organizations with previous experience in offshore wind. [S/T] ▪ Improving confidence in any long-term power procurement contract (PSAs, CPPAs) by i) establishing clear and unambiguous rules, roles, and responsibilities for each of the contracting party; ii) introducing some flexibility in these contracts with a minimum and maximum price range. [S/T]	
Offshore wind finance	▪ Enabling project finance mechanisms, structured on a non-recourse basis in the development phase. Such structures can pool domestic and international capital and broaden the financial market participants to bring in more institutional investors, which can contribute to lower cost of finance. [S/T]	Project developers, lenders, investors
	▪ Organising targeted workshops, knowledge sharing and other capacity building programmes for the financial services industry to improve the understanding of offshore wind market fundamentals in the Philippines. [S/T]	International financial services with offshore wind experience. Debt and Equity advisors
	▪ Leveraging concessional finance for early projects to help the Philippines overcome the initial cost premium for offshore wind as a new technology in the country. This can crowd-in commercial finance for future projects and lower the cost of electricity from offshore wind. [S/T]	International Financial Institutions and Development Banks
	▪ Scaling up the use of dedicated financial instruments, especially those based on first loss guarantees, to incentivise commercial finance and lower the cost of capital. [M/T]	International Financial Institutions
Capacity building	▪ Retraining the local workforce for careers in offshore wind across all the supply chain (advisers, technicians, financiers, government agencies, other support staff), combined with incentives to attract overseas Filipino professionals to bring their international experience. [M/T]	DOE, DOST, Government Agencies, Development Partners

Enabling finance and investments for energy efficiency and conservation in public buildings

The energy efficiency market in the Philippines remains nascent and efforts are underway to promote its benefits to help market scale-up. The Philippines has an indicative target of 24% economy-wide energy savings by 2040 (DOE, 2017[5]). To this end, the government has adopted a strategy to lead by example and promote energy efficiency in public buildings.

Due to their smaller scale and funding, energy efficiency projects differ significantly from utility scale renewable energy projects. While offshore wind entails logistical complexities and large-scale resource deployment, energy efficiency projects for public buildings are bound by the needs and priorities of each local government unit (LGU) and prospective contractors. However, comprehensive planning approaches, streamlining of administrative procedures and capacity building among relevant partners are all important components of a developing an ambitious energy efficiency programme. The following near- and medium-term actions can help to incentivise finance and investments in energy efficiency among LGUs:

- **Establishing clear timelines and pathways to meet national energy efficiency goals within public institutions.** The updated National Energy Efficiency Plan (NEECP) 2023 – 2050 has already introduced clear and time-bound sectoral targets that can guide decision making and create a unified direction for energy efficiency investments in public buildings.
- **Reforming some existing regulatory frameworks and investment time horizons related to energy efficiency projects.** The revision of public procurement rules can be an important mechanism to support energy efficiency projects in public buildings. This can be done through implementing specific carve-outs or revisiting procurement rules to accommodate energy efficiency projects with payback periods exceeding one calendar year, as well as allowing bundled contracts.
- **Signalling commitment to energy efficiency progress through fiscal measures to attract private investment where appropriate**. The government can also carefully evaluate opportunities to increase budget allocation to LGUs for energy efficiency projects. While sound public finances remain a priority, having the technical knowledge and capacity in place within the LGUs is important in the early stages of energy efficiency project deployment.
- **Collaborating with development institutions to leverage technical expertise and facilitate private sector engagement.** International development partners can support LGUs in designing a robust and realistic strategy to improve their access to funding sources. Increased awareness on the available commercial funding and an open dialogue between lenders and energy efficiency developers can help LGUs understand the requirements and conditions of an economically viable project.
- **Building on past success to strengthen the private Energy Service Company (ESCO) market**. The Philippines has a favourable regulatory environment for promoting ESCO models, which can encourage more private sector investment in energy efficiency. Establishing a project pipeline in the public sector via a designated aggregator entity could be a step in the right direction. This can be complemented with continuous capacity building measures, dedicated financing windows for ESCO projects, and potentially an Energy Savings Insurance (ESI) scheme adapted for public buildings.
- **Investing in human capital and upskilling to generate new jobs and create a sustainable local workforce**. Like offshore wind, energy efficiency can also benefit from technical assistance in public awareness programmes, skills and talent development provided by the government and international organisations. This can support the successful implementation of early projects and lay the foundations for further scale up in new projects and LGUs.

Table 3. Energy efficiency and conservation in public buildings: key actions and recommendations

Key topic area	Actions [Timing: Short-term (S/T), Medium-term (M/T)]	Implementer
Enhanced cross-government collaboration and planning	▪ Harmonising planning between agencies, national and local authorities to develop an implementation strategy with relevant stakeholders. Facilitating the creation of working groups on energy efficiency in public buildings, hosted by the DOE. [S/T]	DOE, LGUs, Government Agencies
Regulatory reforms	Revising procurement and accounting rules for public authorities to facilitate energy efficiency projects with payback period spanning several years. [S/T] ▪ Liberalising public procurement restrictions to allow for the provision of mixed contracts such as Energy Performance Contracts (EPCs). [S/T] ▪ Assessing current energy efficiency regulatory regime to evaluate if the sub-sector coverage and standards are compatible with the country's climate ambitions. [M/T]	DOE, International development partners
Access to finance	▪ Evaluating options for increasing public budget allocation for LGUs to ensure capacity and resources are in place for early energy efficiency projects. [S/T] ▪ Formulating a strategy to diversify funding through concessional finance, energy efficiency funds, or capital markets via municipal bonds. [M/T] ▪ Developing dedicated campaigns and training sessions to help LGUs understand lender requirements and build economically viable project proposals. [S/T] ▪ Exploring opportunities to establish a project pipeline for energy efficiency investments in the public sector via a designated aggregator entity. [M/T]	DOE, LGUs, International development partners, Private investors
Data collection and transparency	▪ Synthesising data on energy efficiency potential, performance, payback periods and other parameters for business models and knowledge sharing about energy efficiency benefits. [M/T]	DOE, LGUs, International development partners
Capacity building	▪ Implementing capacity building programmes across the supply chain, such as: policy and regulations, project origination, project implementation, financing and incentives, as well as performance data and analytics. [S/T]	DOE, government, agencies, IFIs
Energy Savings Insurance (ESI)	▪ Building on international experience and allowing MDBs and the financial services industry, authorised by the DOE, to trial ESI for the Philippine LGUs. [S/T] ▪ Considering mainstreaming ESI into the insurance market based on trial results. [M/T]	International development partners, DOE

References

DOE (2022), *Mandatory Implementation of Energy Efficiency and Conservation Programs and the Strict Observance of the GEMP Guidelines*. [3]

DOE (2021), *National Renewable Energy Program*. [4]

DOE (2017), *The Philippines Energy Efficiency and Conservation Roadmap 2017 - 2040*. [5]

Philippines Information Agency (2023), *General Profile of the Philippines*. [1]

World Bank (2022), *A Roadmap for Offshore Wind in the Philippines*. [2]

Note

[1] The first OECD-DOE Workshop on unlocking finance and investment for clean energy in the Philippines took place in Manila, Philippines on 31 May – 1 June 2022. The second OECD-DOE workshop took place in Bohol, Philippines on 24 – 25 November 2022.

1 Introduction: key trends and market developments for renewable energy and energy efficiency and conservation in the Philippines

The Philippines has set a goal to achieve a 35% share of renewable energy in its power generation mix by 2030 and 50% by 2040, up from 22% currently. In parallel, the Philippines aims to reduce its economy-wide energy intensity by 3% over the same period. Achieving these targets will require unlocking USD 337 billion in cumulative investments to 2040. Such investments can deliver strong benefits for the local communities and the overall economy of the Philippines. This includes contributions to the GDP with taxes and additional economic activity, the creation of long-term highly qualified jobs, and the restructuring and development of rural and coastal communities. Ensuring a sound policy framework and investment environment will be essential to mobilise domestic and foreign sources of capital to a level commensurate with the country's clean energy ambitions.

The Philippines has increased efforts to decarbonise its economy in recent years. The country submitted its first Nationally Determined Contribution (NDC) in April 2021, committing to a 75% emission reduction during the period 2020 – 2030, against a business-as-usual scenario. Of this target reduction, 2.71% is unconditional and 72.29% is conditional upon resources provided from developed countries (NEDA, 2023[1]). While the Philippines does not have a net-zero greenhouse gas (GHG) target, its conditional NDC ambition is considered consistent with the 1.5°C limit under the Paris Agreement (Climate Analytics, 2022[2]).

The challenge for the Philippines will be to balance the need for emissions reduction with the need to deliver on economic growth (see Figure 1.1). Philippines is ranked as one of the fastest growing developing markets and the outlook remains positive (S&P Global, 2023[3]). Current government policies focus on high growth and steering the country towards an upper middle-income economy in the coming years (NEDA, 2023[1]). This growth will bring benefits, but it will also put pressure on the power sector where energy demand is forecasted to increase by 7% every year to 2040 (DOE, 2020[4]).

To stay under a 1.5°C compatible pathway, the Philippines power sector, which is currently 58% of country's overall emissions (see Figure 1.2), would need to be a driver for emissions reduction (Climate Analytics, 2022[2]). Renewables are expected to fill in a big gap in the low carbon supply mix. The National Renewable Energy Program (NREP) 2020-2040 includes a non-binding interim target of 35% renewable energy in its generation mix by 2030 and 50% by 2040, more than double today's levels (DOE, 2021[5]).

Alongside the power sector, energy efficiency will also play a key role towards the country's emission reduction goals. Under its first Energy Efficiency and Conservation Plan 2017-40, the Philippines targets a decrease in final energy consumption between 1.2% and 1.9% per year for the residential and commercial sectors (which includes public buildings).

Figure 1.1. GDP growth and CO2 emissions

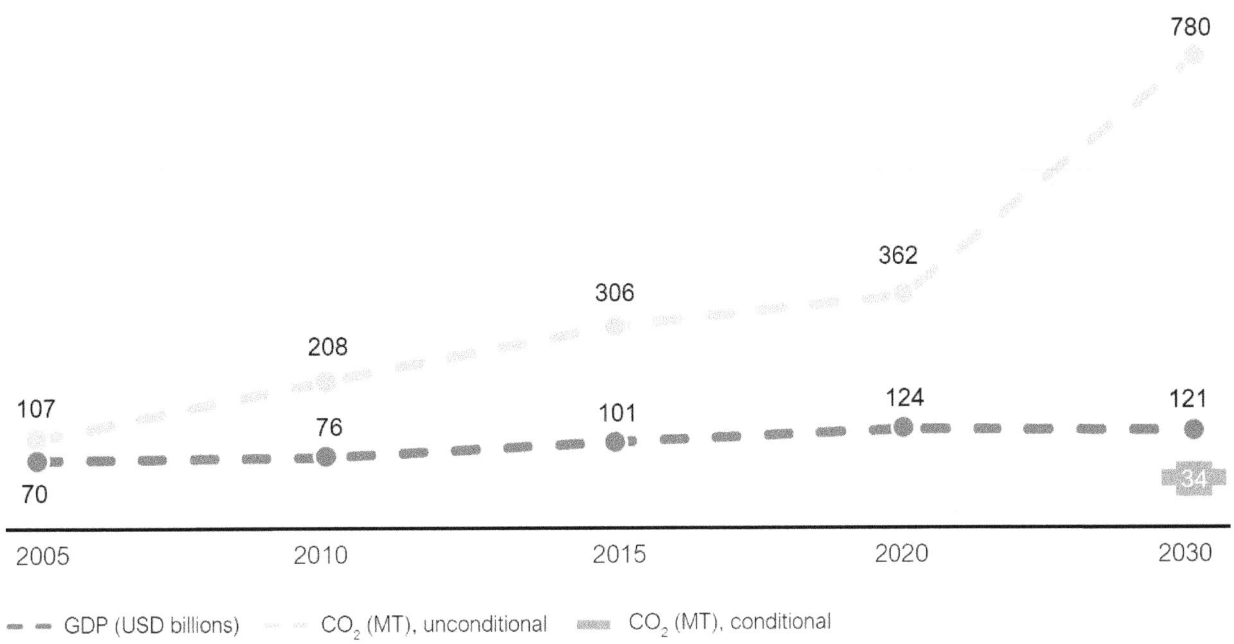

Source: Actuals data from IEA and World Bank statistics 2022, 2030 GDP estimates from S&P 2023, 2030 CO2 emissions from UN

StatLink https://stat.link/27orjb

Figure 1.2. Energy related emissions in the Philippines (in Mt CO_2)

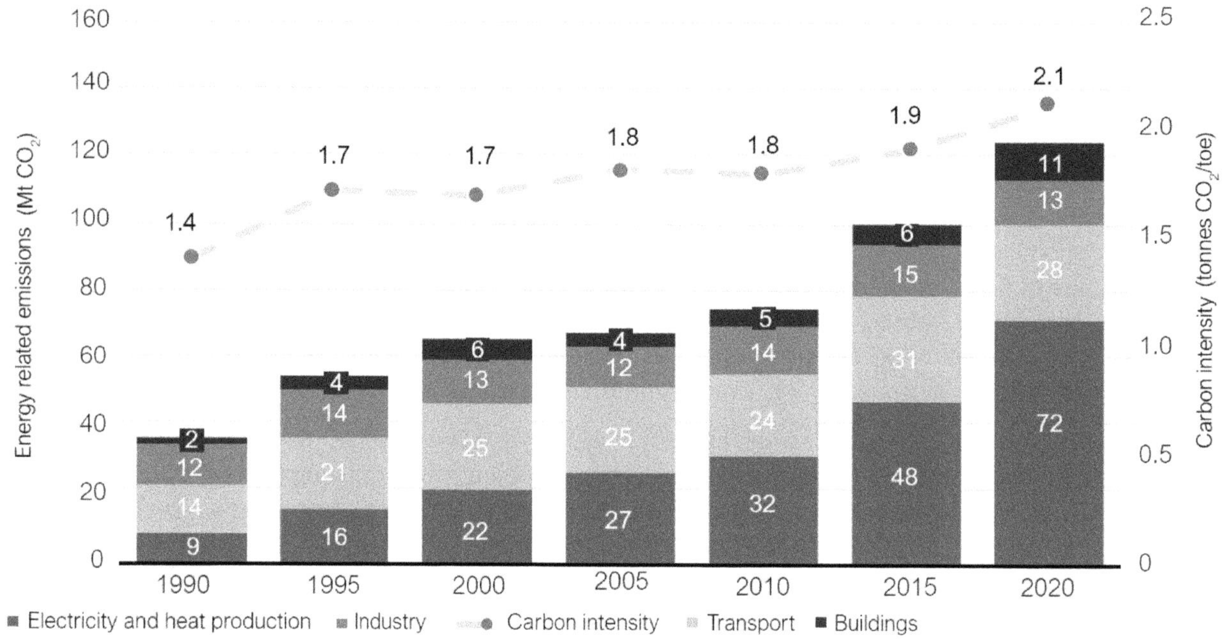

Source: IEA, 2023. World Energy Balances

StatLink https://stat.link/m9ury3

Figure 1.3. Energy related emissions in the Philippines (in %)

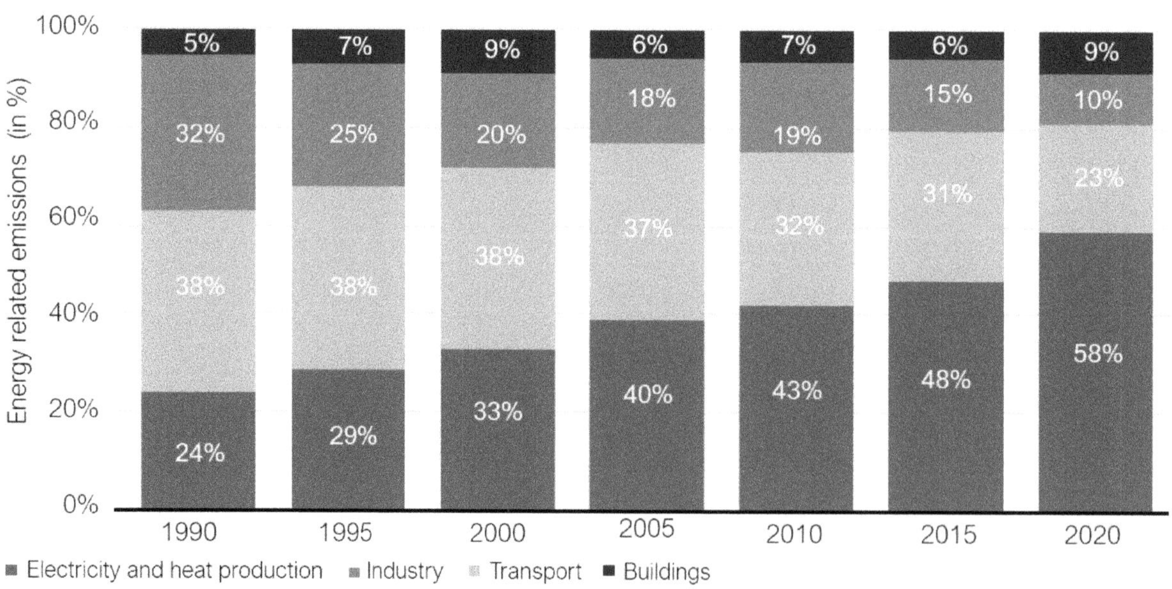

Source: IEA, 2023. World Energy Balances

StatLink https://stat.link/40pqlr

Figure 1.4. The Philippine grid and regional context

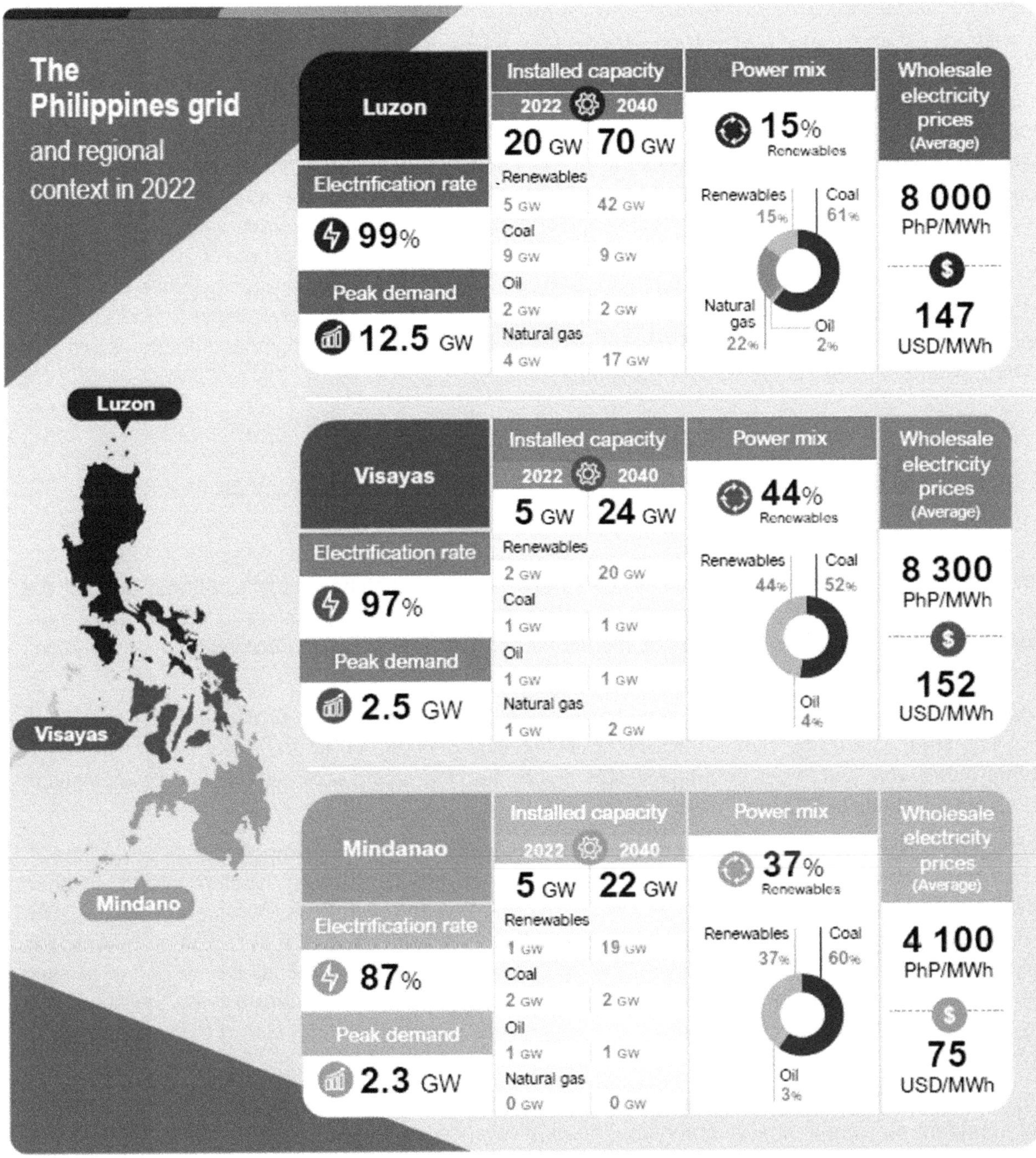

Source: Authors' compilation from IEOMP, 2023; DOE, 2023; IEA Real Time Electricity Tracker, 2023

Box 1.1. The importance of the geographical context in the Philippines

The Philippine power market and its transmission infrastructure need to be considered in the context of the country's unique geography and archipelagic system. A configuration of more than 7,200 islands and the lack of a centralised national grid creates significant regional disparities in quality of service, electrification rate, development stage, and supply/demand management leading to local hotspots, congestion issues and difference in electricity prices (NGCP, 2022[6]). The three main regions in the Philippines are Luzon, Visayas and Mindanao, which all have their separate sub-grids. The grids of Luzon and Visayas islands are interconnected and operate under a unified wholesale electricity market. The island of Mindanao is expected to integrate in the national network in the course of 2023, under the "One Grid 2020" project (NGCP, 2023[7]). It currently operates under its separate wholesale electricity market. Outside the three main grids, transmission infrastructure challenges remain in more than 120 small islands and isolated power grids (Power Philippines, 2023[8]). These regional differences will be reflected, where relevant, in the sections of Chapter 1.

The Philippine power sector under the current National Renewable Energy Programme (NREP) 2020-2040

The three major power sources in the Philippines are coal, renewables and gas. Almost 60% of the electricity supply in the country comes from coal, the largest generation source in the last 20 years. Renewables supply 22% of electricity in the country, but their share has been decreasing over the years. Gas fired power plants provide 18% of electricity supply.

In recent years, the Philippine power sector has been facing concerns over security of supply and affordability, compounded by climate hazards and technical grid issues. In 2021, a total of 107 million consumer-hours were lost to power outages, 10% higher than the record set in 2015 (Philippines Institute for Development Studies, 2023[9]).

The Philippine power sector has become increasingly dependent on fossil fuel imports for its power needs. Over half of the country's primary energy supply is imported (PIDS, 2018[10]). Coal imports have been increasing on average 5% year-on-year in the last three years to reach 30 million tons in 2021 (DOE, 2023[11]) and weigh on the country's annual trade deficit (ILS, 2021[12]). With the depletion of the only gas field in the country, natural gas also faces supply related challenge. As of 2025, all the 10 GW of existing and upcoming gas power plants risk running entirely on imports. This will further expose the country to price volatility and competition for resources in international Liquefied Natural Gas (LNG) markets (IEA, 2023[13]).

Closely linked to the security of supply, are the high electricity prices in the Philippines despite the country having abundant renewable energy potential. The high reliance on fossil fuel imports and a fragmented grid infrastructure that presents challenges for renewable energy integration, have contributed to some of the highest electricity prices in the Philippines (IEA, 2022[14]), compared to other Southeast Asian countries (see Figure 1.6) (Climatescope, 2023[15]). Within the Philippines, issues of affordability and customer capacity to pay can be critical in diesel-based, off-grid areas with some of the most vulnerable population. Inadequate fuel resources to cover demand in these areas can result in the inevitable decision to reduce the service (NPC, 2023[16]).

Figure 1.5. Average electricity prices in the Philippines

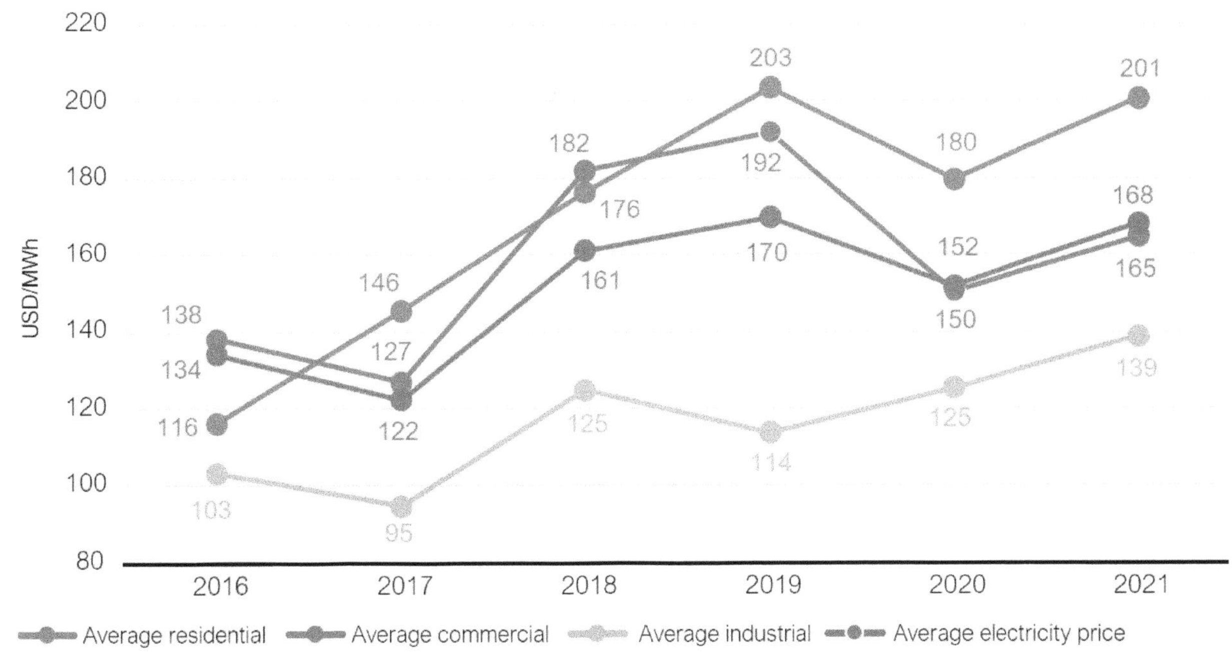

Source: Climatescope 2023

StatLink https://stat.link/a9i6w1

Figure 1.6. Average household electricity prices in Southeast Asia

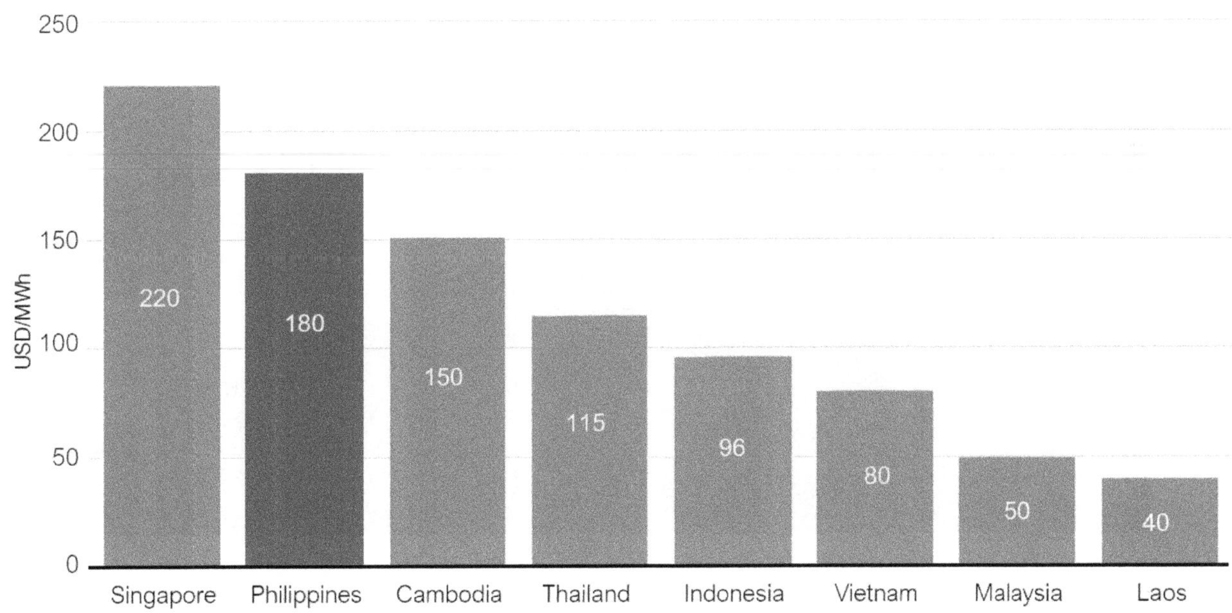

Source: Global Petrol Prices 2023

StatLink https://stat.link/1ts045

To address the security of supply and affordability concerns, the DOE launched the National Renewable Energy Program (NREP) to diversify the power generation mix in the Philippines through a range of low carbon sources by 2040 (DOE, 2021[5]). Under the NREP 2020-2040, the DOE aims for 35% renewables target in the power generation mix by 2030 and 50% target by 2040. To achieve this target, a total of 75 GW of additional renewable energy capacity (10 times the current level) is required by 2040 (DOE, 2021[5]).

Figure 1.7. Generation mix under NREP 2020-2040 (in TWh): 50% RE scenario

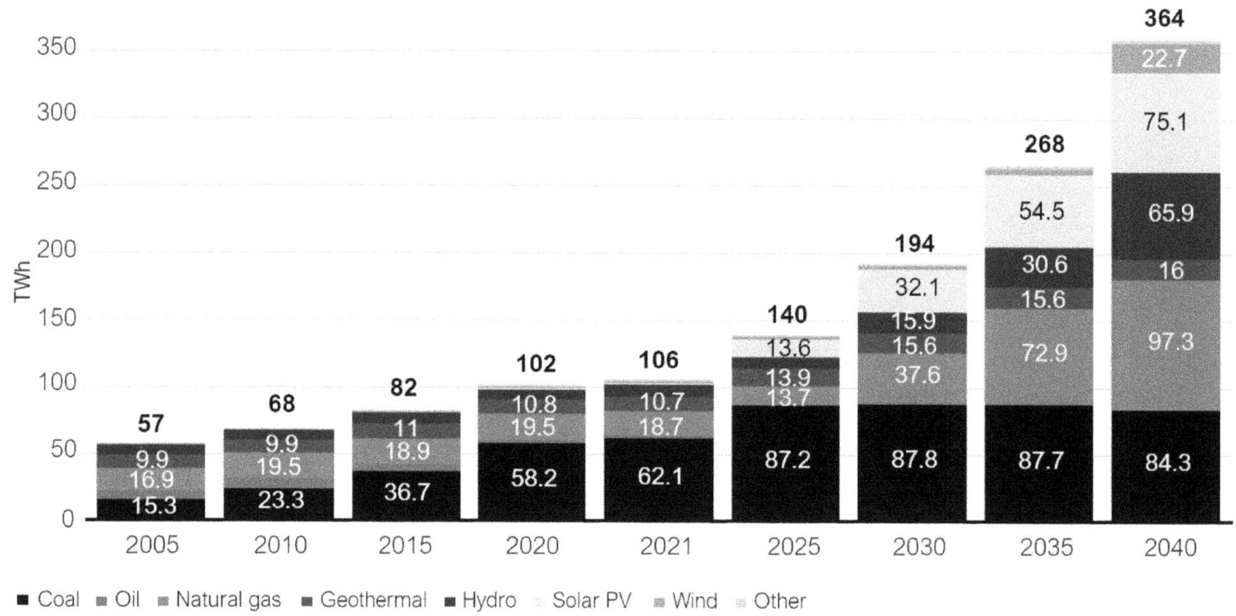

Source: DOE, 2023: NREP 2020 – 2040

StatLink https://stat.link/nkclm8

Figure 1.8. Generation mix under NREP 2020-2040 (in %): 50% RE scenario

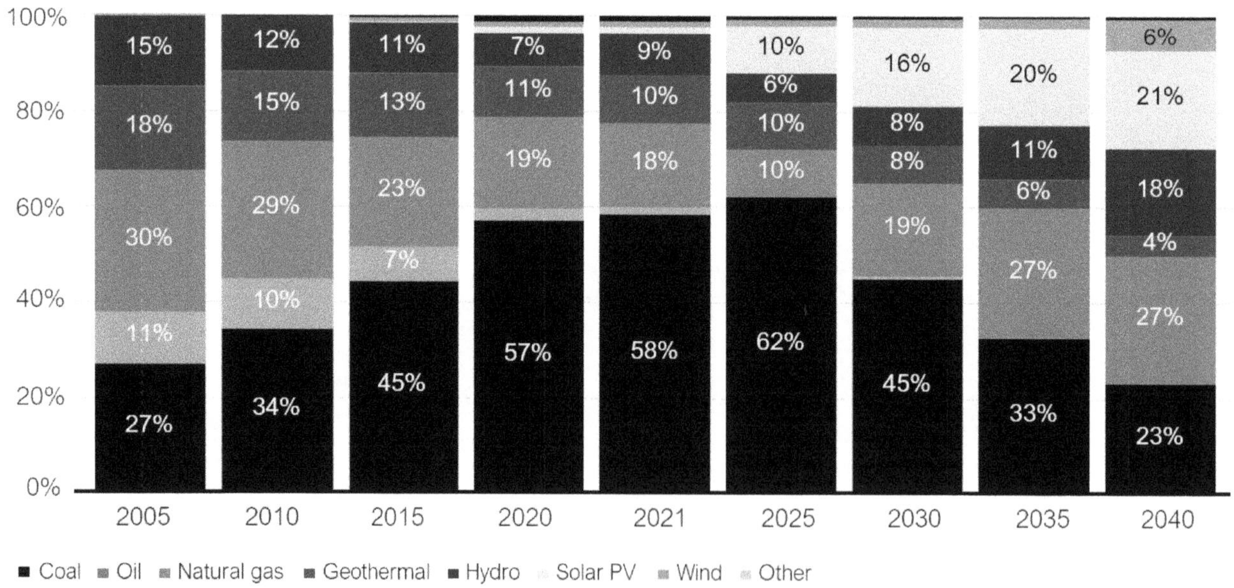

Source: DOE, 2023: NREP 2020 – 2040

StatLink https://stat.link/4oj2km

Figure 1.9. Installed capacity under the NREP 2020-2040 based on 50% RE generation in 2040

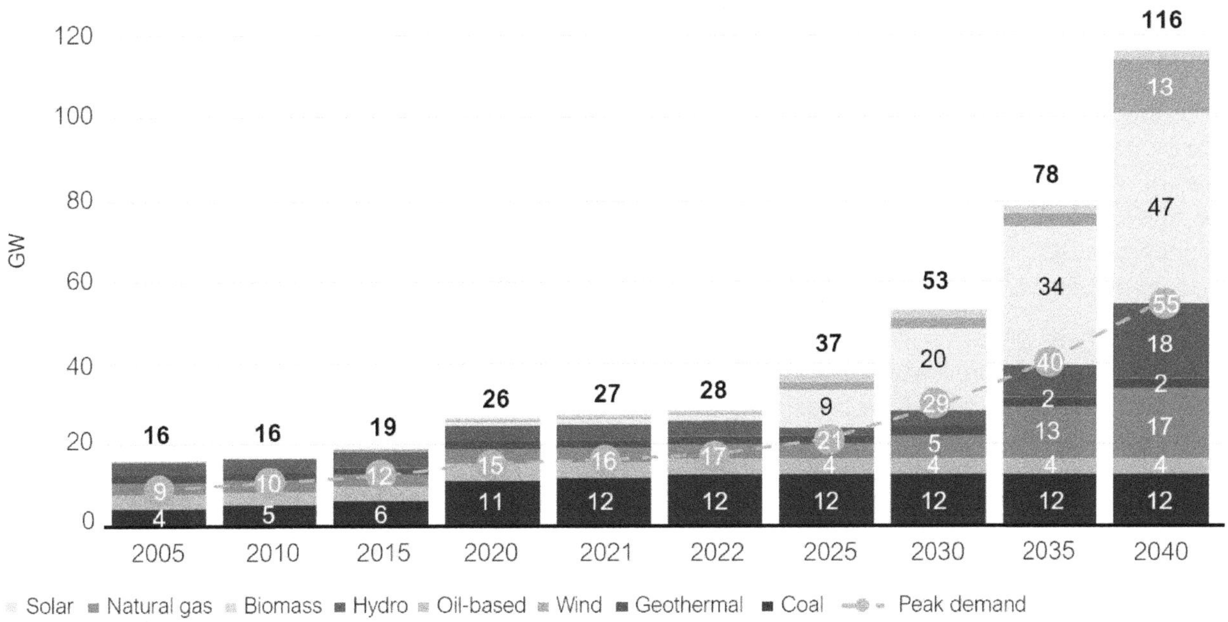

Note: Peak demand excludes 25% reserve rate. NREP not yet updated with offshore wind potential.
Source: DOE, 2023: NREP 2020 – 2040

StatLink https://stat.link/5sh4l3

The Philippines electricity market and institutional context

The Philippines has one of the most liberalised power markets in Southeast Asia (OECD, 2023[17]). The comprehensive Electric Power Industry Reform Act (EPIRA) was enacted in 2001 to restructure the power sector and establish an independent regulator to oversee the market, the Energy Regulatory Committee (ERC). The legislation unbundled generation, transmission, and distribution of electricity, though some cross-ownership can exist between generation and distribution businesses within limits set by the ERC (PIDS, 2018[10]).

Independent Power Producers (IPP) provide most of the generation. For rural areas not connected to the main grid, the mandated electricity provider is the government-owned National Power Corporation (NPC). The Government owns all the transmission assets through the National Transmission Corporation (TransCo), but the operations are managed by the grid concessionaire National Grid Corporation of the Philippines (NGCP), a 40% Chinese owned enterprise. Distribution utilities own and operate the distribution network, where qualified customers can choose their supplier and source of power under the various regulations guaranteeing open access (PIDS, 2018[10]).[1]

Privatisation programmes that followed EPIRA resulted in the creation of wholesale and retail electricity markets. Even though generation in the wholesale market is competitive, most of the electricity (~85%) is traded over the counter (OTC) via bilateral contracts in the form of power supply agreements (PSAs) with a duration of 10 to 25 years (DOE, 2022[18]). The terms are decided privately between the generator and the distributor, except for contracts for the retail captive market. The ERC reserves the right to check the compliance of these contracts with a least-cost approach obligation that follows a competitive selection process (CSP) (World Bank, 2021[19]). The Wholesale Electricity Spot Market (WESM) is the marketplace for buying or selling capacity that is not covered by PSAs.

The opening of the market allowed for new players to enter, yet competition remains limited. There are about 30 independent power producers, but almost 60% of the national installed capacity is concentrated on the balance sheets of the three main players: San Miguel Energy Corp (22% market share), First Gen (17%) and Aboitiz Power (15%).

Similarly, the distribution services sector has over 150 market players, but the majority of operations is concentrated with Meralco (70% market share), mostly in the Luzon grid. The remaining 40% market share consists of a few regional players and over 100 consumer-owned on-grid and off-grid electric co-operatives, which play an important role in serving the archipelagic island configuration. Regional players include VECO – the largest utility in the Visayan grid and the second largest in the Philippines, and Davao Light and Power – the largest utility in the Mindanao grid (DOE, 2023[20]).

To ensure that there will be no monopoly in power generation, the government has enforced market share limits for generators. These limits stand at 25% market share of the national installed generating capacity and 30% market share in any of the three main grids (ERC, 2022[21]).

Figure 1.10. Overview of the Philippines power market and institutional context

Policy and oversight	Department of Energy (DOE)		
	Energy Regulatory Commission (ERC)		
Generation	Public and Private power producers	Generation	Actors include a number of partially or fully integrated generation, distribution, and retail companies.
		Own generation	
Transmission	Public transmission owner & operator	National Grid Corporation of the Philippines	
Distribution	Public and private grid operators	Regulated distribution utilities acting as local natural monopolies in their areas of operation	
Commercialisation	Public and private retail agents	Unregulated Retail Electricity Suppliers	
Markets	Wholesale Electricity Spot Market (WESM)	Bilateral contracts	Market of long-term contracts
		Power Exchange (PE)	Net pool (spot market)
System operations	Independent Electricity Market Operator (IEMOP)		
End users	Regulated and non-regulated	Captive market	Customers (mostly households and small business) who buy energy from retail agents at tariffs regulated by ERC
		Contestable customers	Large customers (beyond 750 Kw) who can negotiate energy contracts freely with generators or trade power in the spot market

Source: OECD Clean Energy Finance and Investment Mobilisation, 2023

Overview of relevant policies, legislation, and regulation in the Philippine energy sector

The Philippines has taken action to reduce reliance on fossil fuels, despite not having a definite phase-out timeline.

- In 2020, the Philippines introduced a ban on new coal power plants, but already approved projects will go through and the Philippines expects another 2.3 GW of new coal capacity to come online by 2027 (IEA, 2022[14]). Some of the early projects have been in operation since 1982 but overall, the current fleet is estimated to have 13 years of operational life remaining. The private sector is already acting on coal asset divestments. As of the first quarter of 2023, two divestments have been announced from two different coal power plants, including both domestic and international investors.[2]
- In 2018, the Philippines introduced higher fuel excise taxes as part of a broader legislation on Tax Reform for Acceleration and Inclusion (TRAIN). To date, this is the only form of carbon pricing available in the Philippines (PIDS, 2018[22]). Meanwhile, all forms of fossil fuel subsidies had already been removed via the industry deregulation through EPIRA (Climatescope, 2023[15]).

In parallel, the Philippines has also taken action to support low carbon generation. In April 2023, an executive order issued by the President, mandates a policy and administrative framework for offshore wind development in the Philippines, including harmonisation in the Energy Virtual One-Stop Shop (EVOSS) (DOE, 2023[23]). This complements already existing measures under the Renewable Energy (RE) Act of 2008, the backbone of the country's strategy for renewable energy deployment (IEA, 2017[24]).

- **Feed in Tariff (FIT)** was one of the early measures introduced under the Act. It supported around 1.4 GW of new renewable energy capacity installed. The FIT was discontinued in 2019, with the exception of run-of-river hydro, a technology still eligible for the tariff. Renewable energy sources still enjoy priority dispatch even after the FIT suspension. The tariff is funded by a fixed charge on all electricity consumers (the FIT-All fund managed by TransCo), except for those customers eligible for subsidies (Climatescope, 2023[15]).
- In 2017, the **Renewable Portfolio Standards (RPS)** policy kicked in to guarantee a revenue stream for the industry by mandating distribution utilities and electricity suppliers to procure or produce a minimum supply generated from renewable energy. Currently this stands at 2.52%, subject to annual revisions where an incremental growth more than 1% on the previous year is foreseen to meet targets and grow the renewable energy market (DOE, 2017[25]).
- The **Green Energy Auction Programme (GEAP)** was introduced in 2021 to help the government achieve its targets, with auction rounds expected to be held annually. The current auction design is organized by technology bands per region, with specific regional targets for hydropower, biomass, solar and wind energy. The first auction was held in June 2022 and awarded almost all the auctioned capacity, a total of 2 GW of renewable energy. The Energy Regulatory Commission (ERC) sets the ceiling price (GEAR – Green Energy Auction Reserves). The winners benefit from 20-year power supply contracts at the awarded strike price, the Green Energy Tariff (GET), which is paid by the FIT-All fund (DOE, 2021[26]).
- Building reliable power systems requires solutions beyond the generation side. As such, the other two measures in the RE Act focus on consumers and the end user more broadly. The **Net Metering Programme (NMP)** incentivises distributed generation by enabling end users to install systems up to 100 KW for own consumption and the ability to sell the surplus power to the grid (DOE, 2023[27]). The **Green Energy Option Programme (GEOP)** gives end users, with average peak demand of 100 KW, the option to choose renewable energy sources for their supply (DOE, 2023[28]).
- In addition to the sector specific policy instruments, the RE Act offers a zero-rated VAT generation charge and a tax exemption for the carbon credits. Renewable energy developers also benefit from

a duty-free importation and special realty tax on equipment and machinery that will be used in building the power plant. These incentives are complemented with a seven-year tax holiday on corporate income, followed by a reduced corporate tax rate thereafter. The general eligibility requirements and screening lies with the Department of Energy (DOE) and the Board of Investments (IEA, 2017[24]).

It should be noted that the measures of the RE Act have several elements that have made the Philippines an attractive market in Southeast Asia. These include:

- the inflation indexed FIT
- a transparent degression FIT rate to reflect technological advances in cost reductions
- and more recently the launch of market-based measures such as auctions and the Renewable Energy Market, which is an important tool for the certificate-based tracking of procured power.

Despite this, the Philippines has only added 3 GW of renewable energy sources in the 14 years since the introduction of the RE Act (DOE, 2022[29]).

- Stakeholder consultations by the OECD highlighted delayed implementation of the initial measures, liquidity issues on the FIT fund's allowance and bottlenecks on grid infrastructure, including smart meter roll-out, as some of the reasons leading to the rather low renewable energy capacity additions (relative to 2030 and 2040 targets).
- Investors also highlighted issues with the competitive selection process (CSP) rules that demand distribution utilities to contract electricity using a least-cost approach. Although a welcome development, the current CSP requirements to classify technologies by mode of operation (baseload, mid-merit, peak) could limit access of variable renewable projects and thereby contravene the CSP's technology neutrality principle. Moreover, they lock power generators and distribution utilities in rigid long-term contracts with very few options to hedge against financial losses (or benefit from high prices) resulting from price volatility. This is reflected in continuous renegotiation of the contractual terms, including prices, which contradict the CSP principles (Barcelona, 2023[7]).[3]

Box 1.2. The FIT and GEAP programmes in the Philippines

The Philippines has transitioned from FIT towards competitive allocation of renewable energy capacity. The country so far has held two auction rounds in 2022 and 2023 respectively. The first auction in 2022 awarded almost all the auctioned capacity, whereas the second auction round in 2023 was largely undersubscribed. Only 3.6 GW of wind and solar PV technologies were awarded, compared to 11 GW offered. This raises questions on the economic viability of the tariffs set by the ERC, supply chain restrictions in global energy markets, delivery timelines for awarded projects and timely access to the transmission grid.

Table 1.1. Summary of FIT and GEAP programmes in the Philippines

	Feed in Tariff			Green Energy Auction Programme				Other design features of FIT and GEAP		
	Total Awarded capacity (MW)	**2010** FIT-1 Rate PHP/KWh (USD/KWh)	**2015** FIT-2 Rate PHP/KWh (USD/KWh)	**2022** Awarded capacity (MW)	**2022** GEAR PHP/KWh (USD/KWh)	**2023** Awarded capacity (MW)	**2023** GEAR PHP/KWh (USD/KWh)	**Tenure**	**Dispatch**	**Price regime***
Solar	427	9.7 (0.17)	8.7 (0.16)	1,490	3.7 (0.07)	2,068	4.3 (0.08)	20	Must	Fixed
Wind	765	8.5 (0.15)	7.4 (0.14)	374	6.1 (0.11)	1,512	5.8 (0.11)	20	Must	Fixed
Biomass	165	6.6 (0.12)	6.6 (0.12)	3	5.1 (0.09)	-	5.4 (0.1)	20	Priority	Fixed
Hydro	40	5.9 (0.11)	5.9 (0.11)	99	5.5 (0.1)	na	na	na	na	Fixed

12-month rolling average of spot market electricity prices in the Philippines in 2023 stands at 7.5 PHP / KWh or 0.14 USD / KWh

*Projects subject to FIT are applicable to a degression rate of 6% from Solar PV technologies, applicable after year one from effectivity of FIT, and 0.5% for the rest of the technologies applicable after year two from effectivity of FIT.

Figure 1.11. Awarded capacity under the FIT and GEAP programmes in the Philippines

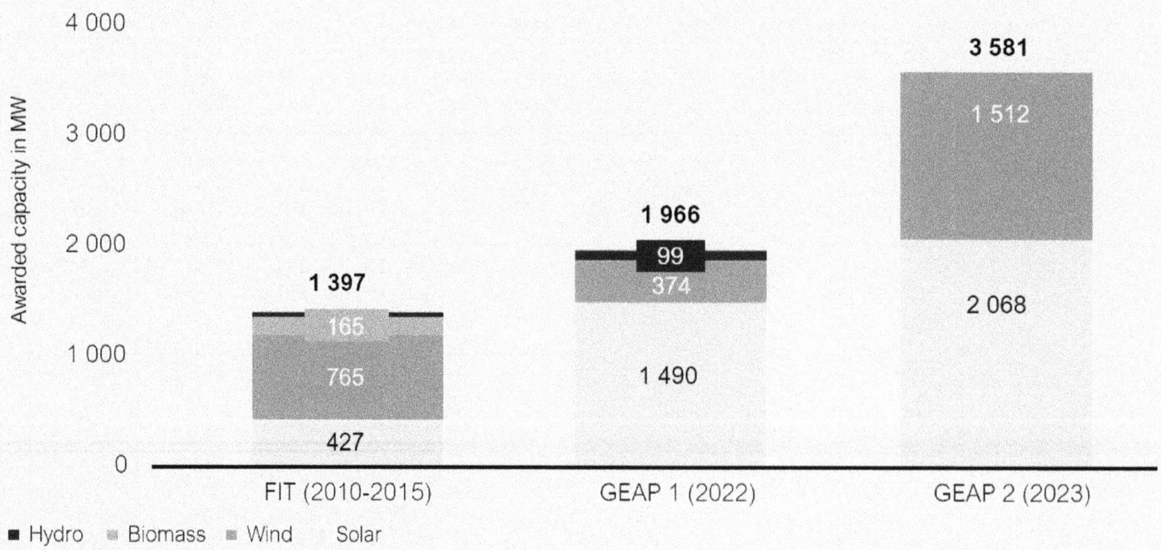

Source: DOE, 2023

Figure 1.12. Tariffs set by the ERC under the FIT and GEAP programmes in the Philippines

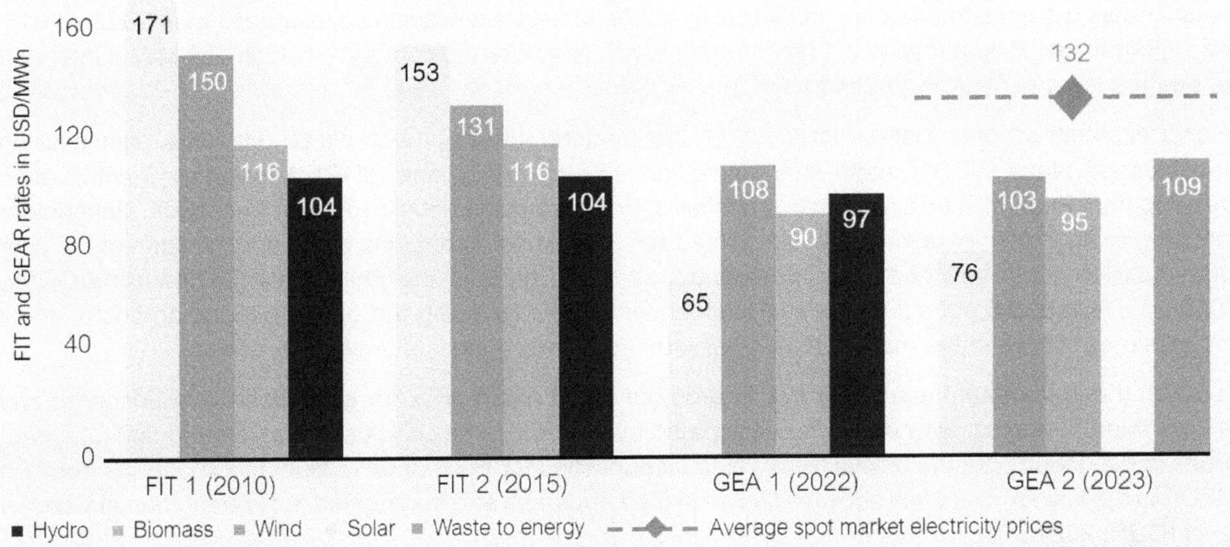

Source: Author's compilation from Simmons & Simmons, 2016; Philippines Institute for Development Studies, 2018; DOE, 2023; TransCo, 2023

StatLink https://stat.link/f1yi0m

Transmission assets and grid infrastructure in the Philippines

The transition to a liberal market resulted in higher electrification coverage in the Philippines. The national average stands at 95.5%, albeit with differences between the three main power grids in the country (see Box 1.1). Outside the main grids, transmission infrastructure challenges remain in more than 120 small islands and isolated power grids (Power Philippines, 2023[8]).

As renewables begin to play a greater role in generation, future spending on grids will be needed to ensure a balanced and secure power supply. In the latest development plan, the NGCP has received over 7 GW of connection requests, mostly in the Luzon region. There are another 35 GW of prospective projects in the pipeline that haven't yet reached financial close. The country's peak demand in the last two years has been around 15 GW but this is expected to quadruple by 2040 (NGCP, 2022[6]).

During OECD stakeholder consultations, investors noted that the current grid connection planning may not be well suited to support the renewable energy market. Under the current planning, grid owners and operators are required to include requests for connection facilities in their annual development plans prior to building the connection line for a power plant. This means that it may take over a year to receive (or not) a grid connection permit, adding uncertainty to the development and construction of renewable energy projects as financing will not be possible without a grid connection approval.

The Competitive Renewable Energy Zone (CREZ) policy was introduced to overcome some of these challenges, notably to align the grid planning and development in areas that optimise the use of the country's renewable resources. The CREZ identifies 25 candidate zones and their associated transmission projects including extensions and upgrades of transmission lines as well as substations and island interconnections (DOE, 2020[30]). These are now adopted in NGCP's latest transmission development plan 2022 – 2040 (NGCP, 2022[6]).

As part of a smarter energy system, DOE and NGCP are also looking at battery energy storage (BESS) to support the integration of more renewables in the grid. Long duration storage can be deployed relatively quickly and serve as backup supply in the event of power interruptions, storage for curtailed power or a dispatchable resource to enhance grid flexibility. In the latest transmission development plan 2022 – 2040, the DOE has identified a total of 2.1 GW storage capacity across the country, of which 450 MW is intended as primary reserve (NGCP, 2022[6]).

Island interconnections feature in most of the sectoral development plans (such as transmission development plans (TDP), island interconnection development plans (IIDP), Missionary Electrification Development Plan (MEDP)). But these plans fall short of providing detailed investment needs, stakeholder mapping or an implementation schedule. More than 2200 km of submarine cable and investments of over USD 3 billion could be needed to interconnect all island grids in the Philippines (Berthau and Cader, 2019[31]). Despite the potential of island interconnections in reducing the power generation costs, these projects may not reach the market in the near term considering the high investment costs.

In 2022, the government enacted a law to promote smart micro-grids for electrification in unserved and underserved areas that will need to be designated by the DOE. The DOE estimates around 900 unserved areas in the country but the official list is yet to be published for the market to launch. Experience from the MEDP in the last six years has shown a lack of unified approach and fragmented implementation at national level (DOE, 2021[32]).

Overview of the potential and policies for energy efficiency and conservation in the Philippines

With a fast-growing population and economy, the Philippines' energy demand is projected to increase by 7% annually to 2040 under a business-as-usual scenario (DOE, 2020[4]). The residential, commercial and public services are almost half of the total final energy consumption (IEA, 2023[33]). Ensuring an efficient use of energy through energy efficiency and conservation measures, can play a key role in limiting energy-related emissions as well as reducing future energy needs (DOE, 2017[34]).

Figure 1.13. Share of total final energy consumption in the Philippines

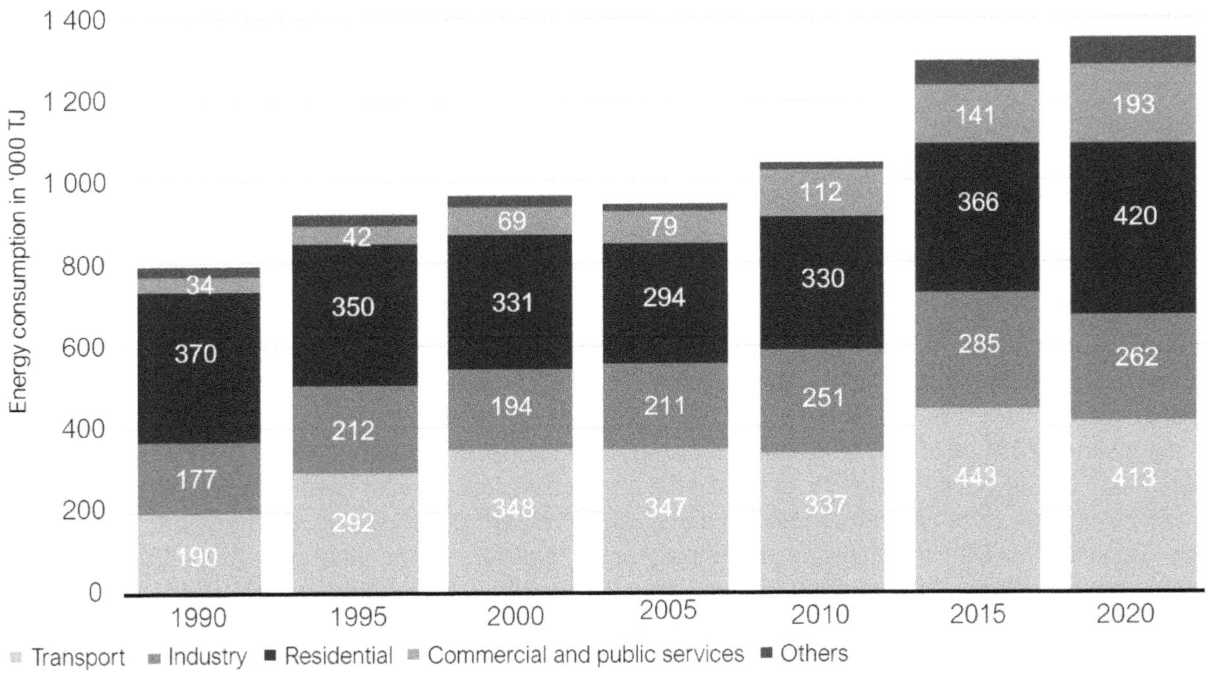

Source: IEA World Energy Balances, 2022

StatLink https://stat.link/5dk9cw

Figure 1.14. Share of total final energy consumption by sector in the Philippines

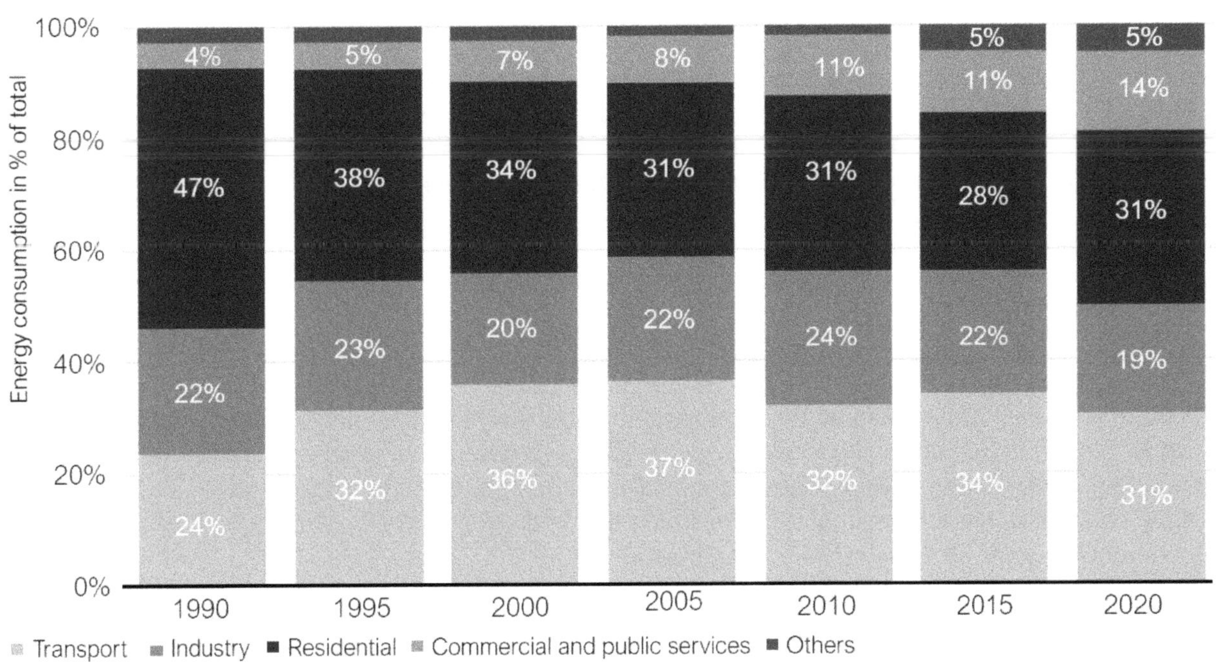

Source: IEA World Energy Balances, 2022

StatLink https://stat.link/3a1t26

To promote energy efficiency in the country, the Department of Energy (DOE) implemented the Republic Act No. 11285 or the Energy Efficiency & Conservation (EE&C) Act in 2019, which covers the residential, industry, commercial and transport sector. The act notably requires the mandatory labelling of products, devices and equipment with the DOE in charge of energy label issuance and its enforcement, monitoring and verification within the local market. Pursuant to the EE&C Act, energy efficiency labels and minimum performance standards cover certain retail household products (room air-conditioners, refrigerators/freezers and lamp ballast). Equally, the EE&C Act encourages all new buildings to be "green buildings" – i.e. to comply with the minimum requirements specified in the 2020 DOE Guidelines on Energy Conserving Design of Buildings. To encourage the adoption of energy efficiency solutions, the act allows for the use of fiscal incentives.[4]

Furthermore, the EE&C Act requires consumers (with an annual consumption above 100,000 kWh) to submit EE&C plans and annual reports, perform energy audits and obtain ISO certifications, as well as hire technical complement to monitor and manage power consumption, among others. Important action has also been taken for public buildings. The Government Energy Management Program (GEMP), which is in place since 2004, is the government-wide program which aims to reduce the monthly energy and fuel consumption of the public sector by at least 10 %, benchmarked against average consumption in 2004 and 2005. With the passage of the EE&C Act, the GEMP covers the whole government sector consisting of the legislative branch, national government agencies, judicial branch, local government units (LGUs), foreign service posts, government-owned and -controlled corporations (GOCCs), constitutional commissions and state universities and colleges. Likewise, the EE&C Act created the Inter-Agency Energy Efficiency and Conservation Committee (IAEECC) to provide strategic direction in the implementation of the GEMP and to evaluate and approve Government Energy Efficiency Projects (GEEPs). Further, it also mandates the LGUs to develop and implement Local EEC Plans that are consistent with the national development plan.

Much like the 2008 RE Act, the 2019 EE&C Act also proposes a number of incentives for energy efficiency projects, the implementation of which is still pending. These incentives include investment support for up to 10 million pesos (around USD 0.18 mln) towards total investment cost, for both new and expansion-related projects. Moreover, the classification of energy efficiency as both Tier-2 and Tier-3 under the Corporate Recovery and Tax Incentives for Enterprises (CREATE) Act also makes these projects eligible for income tax holidays (5-7 years) and duty-free equipment importation. Non-fiscal incentives like Excellence Awards are being given to several categories of establishments (including government) to recognise outstanding performance on energy efficiency.

Investment policies and renewable energy finance trends

Investment policies in the Philippines

In 2020, Philippines was ranked as the third most restrictive country for Foreign Direct Investment (FDI), out of 84 countries ranked by the OECD (OECD, 2023[35]). A series of legal acts mostly related to local content requirements and minimum paid up capital have contributed to this high restrictiveness index. To improve competitiveness, investments, job creation and knowledge transfer, the government has initiated amendments to some of these restrictive legal acts.

In the renewable energy sector, the 40% cap on foreign ownership was removed in November 2022. Foreign investors can now have full ownership in the exploration, development and utilisation of renewable energy sources in the country (solar, wind, hydro and tidal). This also applies to existing projects, where foreign investors can acquire the shares of their local counterparts (DOE, 2022[36]). The power sector is not directly impacted by other administrative local content requirements, mostly related to retail trade and labour practices (Baker McKenzie, 2022[37]).

In February 2023, the Department of Trade and Industry launched the Green Lanes programme to speed up entry of strategic investments into the Philippines. This represents a comprehensive government initiative to improve the overall ease of doing business by expediting, streamlining, and automating government processes specifically for strategic investments, including those in renewable energy (DTI, 2023[38]).

The local content changes have already prompted investment pledges from private investors[5] and technical assistance programmes from foreign governments.[6] The Danish fund – Copenhagen Infrastructure Partners – becomes the first 100% foreign owned company to explore offshore wind in the Philippines through awarded Wind Energy Service Contracts (WESCs) for three projects and a total of 2 GW capacity.

Trends in renewable energy finance in the Philippines[7]

Since 2010, the Philippines has invested a total of USD 11 bln in renewable energy projects (Clean Energy Pipeline, 2023[39]). The regulatory framework and the support measures implemented under the RE Act since 2008 have helped the market, but they have fallen short of mobilising investments needed to meet the 2030 country ambitions (as per the PDP 2020 – 2040). The Philippines aims for an additional 23 GW grid connected renewable energy capacity between now and 2030, that will require over USD 26 billion in finance. With the current spending rate and an access to finance which is below global average (IEA, 2021[40]), the Philippines may not be able to fund the 2030 capacity build-out on domestic resources alone. The size of the financial market in the Philippines is smaller than that of other emerging economies in Asia (IMF, 2022[41]).

Figure 1.15. Investments in new renewable energy projects in the Philippines 2010 – 2022 (includes BESS)

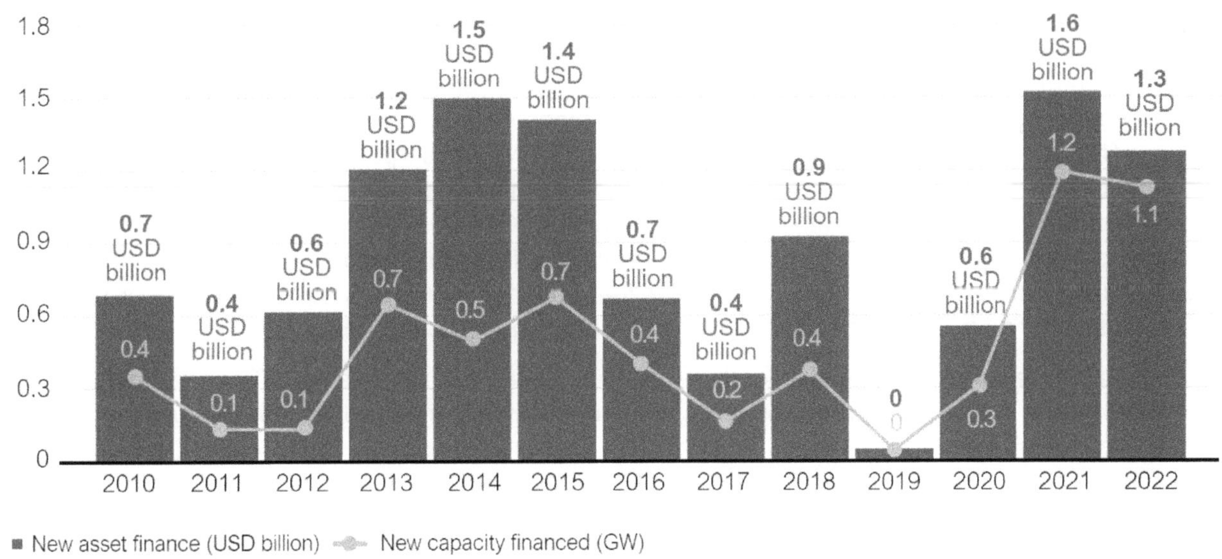

Source: Clean Energy Pipeline, 2023. Includes estimates for undisclosed values. Note that new capacity financed is different from the installed capacity. New capacity financed includes projects that have reached Final Investment Decisions or Financial Close and are still under construction.

StatLink https://stat.link/upqbwk

The Philippine banking sector, which has provided most of the clean energy finance so far (Clean Energy Pipeline, 2023[39]) is concentrated in a handful of banks. The top five banks in the country, all domestic, hold 60% of the banking assets. Most of the large domestic banks are interconnected with non-financial corporations in local-family-owned mixed conglomerates (IMF, 2022[41]). Through their various subsidiaries in infrastructure, power sector, banking and investment funds, these conglomerates have financed over half of the renewable energy capacity in the Philippines. They are de facto the project sponsors and the debt providers in the large infrastructure projects in which they participate. To limit exposure, Bangko Sentral ng Pilipinas (BSP) has enacted boundaries on intracompany lending to 15% of the bank's total loan portfolio (IMF, 2022[41]).

Overseas lenders have a limited presence in the Philippines, holding just 7% of the banking assets in the country (IMF, 2022[42]). Looking at transactional project data from the last 10 years, it can be noted that international banks have participated in transactions jointly with local counterparts in projects where the supply chain has an international element, either equipment or ownership. Despite Philippine companies owning most of the generating assets, the wind energy supply chain draws interest from many international players.[8] The solar sector, however, is more weighted toward regional participants rather than global multinationals (Clean Energy Pipeline, 2023[39]).

Liquidity is not considered to be an issue as banks in the Philippines are well capitalised (IMF, 2022[41]). Clean energy technologies have been financed with a complete range of debt, equity and grant based products mainly from foreign governments. Sovereign government guarantees are no longer an option after the market liberalisation under EPIRA (IMF, 2022[41]). The choice of financial instruments will largely be determined by the profile of developers and project owners. For the big conglomerates, with strong balance sheet positions and long credit history, access to finance is not an issue. They tend to finance most of their projects on balance sheet via debt raised at corporate level (Clean Energy Pipeline, 2023[39]).

Where ticket size is large enough and the profile of developers is diverse enough, project finance has been successfully deployed. The Philippines based power producers will usually take the projects through development before raising capital for construction, where they bring in other shareholders and arrange the debt facility. In the same transaction, loan syndication has incorporated dual currency debt financing from local and international banks. Local banks bring the understanding of the domestic market, with their international counterparts supporting the creation of a supply chain (Clean Energy Pipeline, 2023[39]).

Stakeholders noted that the average loan duration in the Philippines is between 7-8 years and debt covenants tend to be more flexible with local banks. However, project finance transactions for onshore wind have secured up to 15-year long tenors for leverages of around 60-70% (Clean Energy Pipeline, 2023[39]). This is also thanks to Export Credit Agencies (ECA), whose participation has been tied to the sale of components or the provision of foreign capital. ECAs have shouldered transaction related risks for up to 80% of the debt facility, but with potential to go higher (OECD, 2022[43]). Transaction de-risking has also been provided by development banks and multilateral financial institutions. Driven by additionality principles, they have been lifting some of the risk that commercial lenders cannot assume or providing finance for smaller developers who cannot access the big banks (Clean Energy Pipeline, 2023[39]).

Stakeholders noted that commercial lending plays a lesser role in energy efficiency finance. The small-scale nature of energy efficiency projects, and the absence of asset pooling and securitisation in the market lead to high transactional costs, which in turn create limitations for large lenders, investors and development banks. The Philippines has around 500 small thrift banks and rural and co-operative banks (IMF, 2022[41]). Despite this, access to finance for individuals remains low, as indicated in an OECD survey with country stakeholders conducted in 2022. Stringent loan screening criteria and high margins for retail customers lead to energy efficiency projects financed with full upfront equity. At retail level, there is also a lack of demand and to some extent lack of dedicated financial instruments tailored to households and individual loans.

Clean energy finance in the Philippines has equally benefitted from capital market instruments. Initial Public Offerings (IPO) in the Philippines stock exchange for pure renewable energy companies and corporate green bonds have successfully raised equity (Clean Energy Pipeline, 2023[39]). The Philippines is the third largest issuer of green bonds in the Southeast Asian region, with private companies having a prominent role in their issuing, alongside multilateral development banks (MDBs). Currently, the government has not issued any green bonds (Clean Energy Pipeline, 2023[39]). The Asian Development Bank has pioneered considerable financial engineering in clean energy transactions. These include project bonds via the Climate Bonds Initiative (CBI), guarantees via the Credit Guarantee and Investment Facility (CGIF), and most recently the Energy Transition Mechanism (ETM) for the financing of coal phase-out.

Other segments of the Philippine financial system are less developed than other Asian peers. Non-bank financial institutions such as insurance companies, pensions and mutual funds, have a small presence compared to global averages (IMF, 2022[41]).

Figure 1.16. Clean energy finance transactions 2010 – 2022 (bln USD)

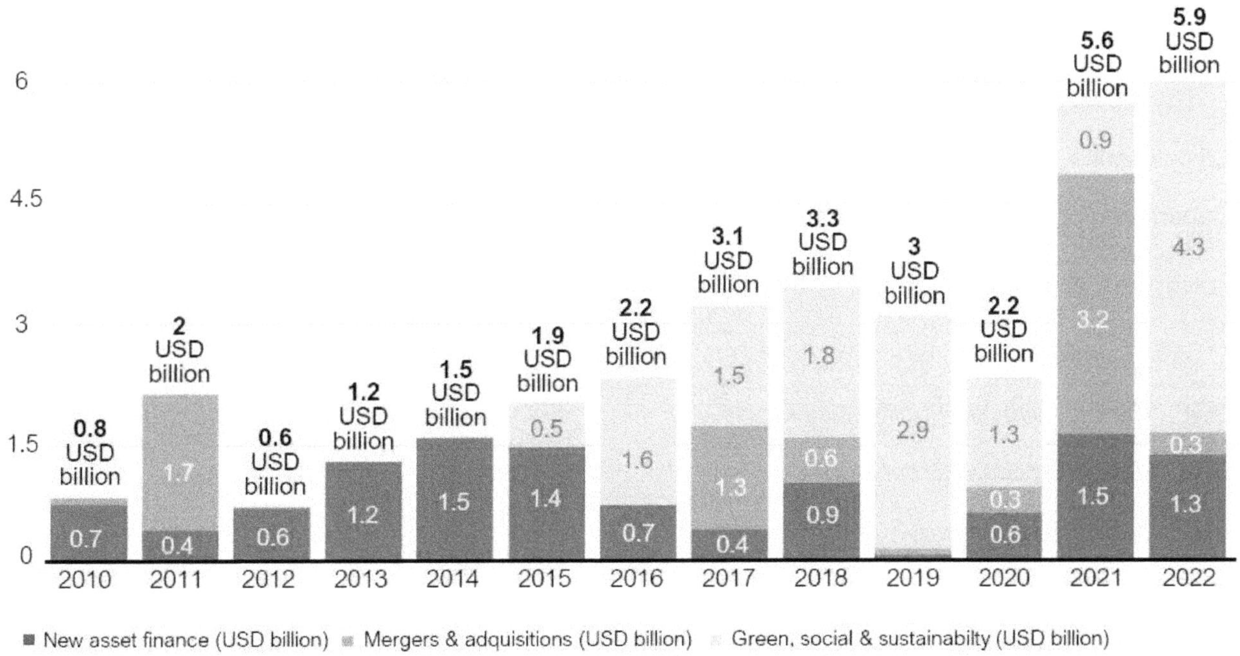

Source: Clean Energy Pipeline, 2023

StatLink https://stat.link/xvgsk5

While availability of capital has not been an issue, it is highly concentrated in the hands of a select few local companies with mixed ownership structures and conglomerate linkages. This may pose limitations to the financing of future renewable energy capacity, especially with rising interest rates and a globally fragile banking sector. Even though the Philippines has limited exposure to overseas lenders, there still are international spillovers from global events (IMF, 2022[41]). In 2023, the Government of the Philippines announced a merger between the Development Bank of the Philippines and the state-owned Landbank (Department of Finance, n.d.[44]), indicating scope for banking consolidation in the market.

References

Baker McKenzie (2022), *Philippine Department of Trade and Industry issues the implementing rules and regulations of the Retail Trade Liberalization Act as amended by Republic Act No. 11595*. [37]

Berthau, P. and C. Cader (2019), *Electricity sector planning for the Philippine islands: considering centralised and decentralised supply options*, Elsevier, https://www.sciencedirect.com/science/article/pii/S0306261919310670. [31]

Clean Energy Pipeline (2023), *Philippine New Asset Finance*. [39]

Climate Analytics (2022), *1.5°C National Pathways Explorer*, https://1p5ndc-pathways.climateanalytics.org/. [2]

Climatescope (2023), *The Philippines*. [15]

Department of Finance (n.d.), *Landbank-DBP merger to strengthen resilience of PH financial sector*, https://www.dof.gov.ph/landbank-dbp-merger-to-strengthen-resilience-of-ph-financial-sector/#:~:text=28%2F03%2F23-,Landbank%2DDBP%20merger%20to%20strengthen%20resilience%20of%20PH%20financial%20sector,serve%20the%20country's%20development%20needs. [44]

DOE (2023), *Distribution Utility (DU) Profile*. [20]

DOE (2023), *Executive Order No.21*. [23]

DOE (2023), *Green Energy Option Program*. [28]

DOE (2023), *Key energy statistics*. [11]

DOE (2023), *Net Metering Home*. [27]

DOE (2022), *40th Electric Power Industry Reform Act (EPIRA) Implementation Status Report*. [18]

DOE (2022), *Department Circular Prescribing Amendments to Section 19 of the RE Law IRR*. [36]

DOE (2022), *DOE Power Statistics*. [29]

DOE (2021), *Green Energy Auction Program in the Philippines*. [26]

DOE (2021), *Missionary Electrification Development Plan*. [32]

DOE (2021), *National Renewable Energy Program*. [5]

DOE (2020), *Power Development Plan 2020 - 2040*, https://www.doe.gov.ph/electric-power/power-development-plan-2020-2040?withshield=1 (accessed on April 2023). [4]

DOE (2020), *Ready for Renewables - Grid Planning and Competitive Renewable Energy Zones (CREZ) in the Philippines*. [30]

DOE (2017), *Renewable Portfolio Standards (RPS)*. [25]

DOE (2017), *The Philippines Energy Efficiency and Conservation Roadmap 2017 - 2040*. [34]

DTI (2023), "E.O. 18 Green Lanes launched to speed up entry of Strategic Investments into the Philippines", *Department of Trade and Industry*, https://www.dti.gov.ph/archives/news-archives/e-o-18-green-lanes-launched-speed-up-entry-strategic-investments-philippines/. [38]

ERC (2022), *A resolution setting the installed generating capacity and market share limitation per grid and national grid for 2022.* [21]

IEA (2023), *Electricity Market Report 2023.* [13]

IEA (2023), *Energy consumption in the Philippines.* [33]

IEA (2022), *Southeast Asian Energy Outlook.* [14]

IEA (2021), *Financing Clean Energy Transitions in Emerging and Developing Economies.* [40]

IEA (2017), *Renewable Energy Act.* [24]

ILS (2021), *Just Transition to Low-Carbon And Climate Resilient Industries: Energy Sector.* [12]

IMF (2022), *Philippines Financial Sector Assessment Program*, https://www.imf.org/en/Publications/CR/Issues/2022/06/02/Philippines-Financial-Sector-Assessment-Program-Technical-Note-on-Macroprudential-Policy-518572 (accessed on 2023). [41]

IMF (2022), *Philippines: Financial sector assessment program.* [42]

NEDA (2023), *Philippines Development Plan 2023 - 2028.* [1]

NGCP (2023), *NGCP One-Grid*, https://www.ngcp.ph/mvip/. [7]

NGCP (2022), *Transmission Development Plan 2022-2040.* [6]

NPC (2023), *National Power Corporation.* [16]

OECD (2023), *Clean Energy Finance and Investment Mobilisation.* [17]

OECD (2023), *OECD Statistics FDI Restrictiveness.* [35]

OECD (2022), *OECD Clean Energy Finance and Investment Consultation Workshop*, https://www.oecd.org/environment/cc/cefim/philippines/secondoecd-doeworkshopunlockingfinanceandinvestmentforcleanenergyinthephilippines.htm (accessed on 2023). [43]

Philippines Institute for Development Studies (2023), *Consumer hours lost to brownouts up 10%*, https://www.pids.gov.ph/details/news/in-the-news/consumer-hours-lost-to-brownouts-up-10 (accessed on 7 February 2023). [9]

PIDS (2018), *Assessment of TRAIN's Coal and Petroleum Excise Taxes.* [22]

PIDS (2018), *Policy Notes: The Philippine electric power industry under EPIRA.* [10]

Power Philippines (2023), *Power Philippines News.* [8]

S&P Global (2023), "Philippines economy shows strong expansion", *S&P Global Market Intelligence*, https://www.spglobal.com/marketintelligence/en/mi/research-analysis/philippines-economy-shows-strong-expansion-jan23.html#:~:text=Over%20the%20next%20decade%20the,growth%20in%20urban%20household%20incomes (accessed on 25 January 2023). [3]

World Bank (2021), *Philippines Electric Power Industry Reform Act of 2001*. [19]

Notes

[1] Retail Competition and Open Access (RCOA) mechanism and the Green Energy Option Programme (GEOP) are two measures that allow corporate sourcing of power in the Philippines.

[2] ETM coal divestment project in collaboration with ACEN and a South Korean investor announcing another coal divestment.

[3] San Miguel Corporation Global and Meralco seeking rate hikes in their contracts to cover losses on fuel costs due to high global coal prices natural gas supply restrictions from the Malampaya gas field. https://powerphilippines.com/ca-nullify-erc-ruling-on-meralco-smc-rate-hike/.

[4] The DOE issued Department Circulars DC2021-05-0011 and DC2022-03-0004 which establishes the procedures and criteria for the evaluation, approval, and endorsement of EE projects and strategic investments to the Board of Investments (BOI) for the eligibility under these fiscal incentives.

[5] Chinese investors commit USD 14 bln in power sector investments in the Philippines; Philippines – Japan consortium is formed to explore renewable energy technology developments; Danish Fund, Copenhagen Infrastructure Partners, amongst others.

[6] DOE has secured technical assistance from the government of the United Kingdom to address development issues for offshore wind projects in the Philippines.

[7] Unless otherwise stated, this chapter is based on author's analysis from Clean Energy Pipeline financial transactions in the Philippines since 2008. This includes new asset finance, refinancing transactions, mergers and acquisitions and capital market transactions. To the extent possible, transactions capture all clean energy technologies in the Philippines, including storage and self-generation. Energy efficiency transactions are not included.

[8] Mainstream Renewable Power, Acciona, Siemens, Iberdrola, WPD, Vestas, Macquaire, Copenhagen Infrastructure Partners, Total and Shell are some of the international companies present in the onshore wind supply chain and the upcoming offshore wind projects.

2 Mobilising finance and investment for offshore wind

The Philippines is estimated to have an offshore wind potential of 178 GW, none tapped so far. With high and more consistent wind speeds and a reduced environmental impact, offshore wind can be a key technology for the country's energy transition. Offshore wind for the Philippines offers the prospect of better utilising the country's maritime resources. This can bring additional investments in the local economy such as ports and infrastructure upgrades, direct and indirect jobs, as well as re-skilling and knowledge transfer. This chapter identifies areas for collaborative actions among policy makers, the industry, and financiers to build the country's offshore wind market.

Offshore wind growth potential and investment needs

The World Bank estimates that offshore wind projects in the Philippines may require capital expenditure in the range of USD 7.5-50 billion by 2040, depending on the level of ambition which was estimated at between 5.6 and 40.5 GW installed capacity (World Bank, 2022[1]). (Box 2.1) In the Power Energy Plan (PEP) 2023 – 2050, currently under discussion, the DOE is looking at developing between 19 - 50 GW of offshore wind. In line with this ambition, six potential offshore wind development zones have been identified, mostly for floating technologies.

Box 2.1. The World Bank Roadmap on offshore wind in the Philippines

The World Bank estimates that offshore wind in the Philippines has a technical resource potential of 178 GW and the possibility to supply 23% of the country's electricity by 2050. While some of these resources are found in shallow waters close to population demand centres, the vast majority (about 90%) are in waters deeper than 50 metres, suggesting floating offshore wind as a more suitable alternative for deep waters. In addition to helping the Philippines achieve its climate commitment of peak greenhouse gas emissions by 2030, offshore wind is increasingly seen as a potential source of economic growth, job creation and energy security. With higher capacity factors compared to other renewable energy technologies, reduced competition for land resources, infrastructure upgrades for ports and roads, re-skilling and knowledge transfer in local and often rural communities, offshore wind can help deliver an inclusive and just energy transition (World Bank, 2022[2]). Conscious of the role offshore wind can have in the low carbon transition, the Government is expected to include long term resource-specific capacity or generation targets for offshore wind in the upcoming revisions to the Philippine Energy Plan in 2023 (DOE, 2022[3]).

Table 2.1. World Bank indicators under the Low Growth and High Growth offshore wind scenarios

	Low Growth Scenario	High Growth Scenario
Capacity installed (by 2050)	5.6 GW	40.5 GW
Electricity share (by 2050)	3.3%	23%
Jobs (by 2040)	15,000 FTE years	205,000 FTE years
Local content (by 2040)	20%	35%
Gross value added (by 2040)	USD 1.1 billion	USD 14 billion
Capital expenditure (by 2040)	USD 7.5 billion	USD 50 billion
Infrastructure investment needs	None	Significant
Fixed LCOE (in 2030)	USD 77 per MWh	USD 76 per MWh
Floating LCOE (in 2040)	USD 61 per MWh	USD 47 per MWh
Turbines installed (by 2040)	150	1000

Note: FTE = Full-time equivalent; LCOE = Levelised cost of electricity; MWh = Megawatt-hour
Source: (World Bank, 2022[2])

Like most infrastructure projects, offshore wind is capital intensive. In 2021, new offshore wind projects saw an average global capital cost of USD 2,858/kW, 41% below the 2010 level. New plants in Asia and Europe were on average on par with this global weighted average value (IRENA, 2022[4]). Given the large scale of investment that needs to be spent upfront, the cost and availability of finance can be a significant hurdle, especially if risks related to technology, policy and markets are not carefully managed. Any risk mitigation in financial structuring to unlock low-cost capital will require a thorough understanding of the risks associated with offshore wind projects in the Philippines and correct pricing of these risks from the party best placed to capture them.

Offshore wind market and policy developments

The government of the Philippines is progressing quickly to establish the market rulebook for the country's future offshore wind industry. Several Executive Orders have been issued to speed up offshore wind market development and more broadly strategic investments.

In November 2022, the President of the Philippines approved a proposal made by the Department of Energy (DOE) to explore and develop the Philippines' offshore wind potential to improve energy security. The President's approval empowers the DOE to fast-track the policy, regulatory and market developments for offshore wind.

In April 2023, the President issued another executive order to set up the "Offshore Wind Development and Investment Council", a one-stop shop for offshore wind comprising 10 government agencies. This is expected to accelerate and streamline permitting, update approval procedures for offshore wind projects, and improve interagency co-ordination (DOE, 2023[5]). This would eventually be integrated into the Energy Virtual One-Stop Shop (EVOSS) platform, a web-based monitoring system for energy applications in the Philippines (EVOSS, 2023[6]).

Some of the first steps taken by the DOE to support the development of offshore wind capacity in the country include customising and streamlining the regulatory environment for projects. A series of public consultations has been launched to revise the "Omnibus Guidelines" that govern the administration of renewable (wind) energy service contracts.

As of September 2023, the DOE had awarded 79 wind energy service contracts (WESCs) to offshore wind developers, representing plans for a maximum cumulative capacity of 62. The DOE indicated that several Letters of Intent (LOI) proposing further offshore wind projects have been sent by international developers following the government's decision to relax foreign ownership limitations on renewable energy projects in 2022, suggesting a strong outlook for offshore wind in the Philippines.

Current offshore wind service contracts (WESCs) are at different stages of pre-development activities. The earliest of these contracts are expected to come online by 2028. Some early development stage projects are in the wind resource measurement phase whereas other projects have been endorsed by the DOE and NGCP for grid System Impact Studies (SIS) to assess the impact of the proposed plants on the current grid infrastructure.

In December 2023, the first offshore wind project in the Philippines received clearance by the Board of Investments (BOI) for an expedited treatment under the country's Green Lane programme. The 450 MW Frontera Bay Wind Power Project, off the coast of Cavite, is expected to cost around USD 1.5 billion. The project is expected to be operational in 2028 and will create 2700 local jobs in its pre-development, development, and operational phases, while providing training and development to local communities (BusinessWorld, 2023[7]).

Box 2.2. Ongoing international technical assistance programmes in the Philippines

Several international partners are assisting key institutions in the Philippines to establish the right policies and incentives, drawing on global best practices and regulatory conditions across the offshore wind supply chain. In particular:

- The World Bank and DOE jointly launched the "Offshore Wind Roadmap of the Philippines" in April 2022, which identifies the technical resource potential, two growth scenarios, and a wide range of recommendations to accelerate offshore wind development in the Philippines. Following the publication of the Roadmap and building on its recommendations, the World Bank is currently providing a package of technical assistance supporting transmission infrastructure planning and environmental regulatory updates. These will be in line with international standards and take into account the specific geographical profile of the country.
- The Asian Development Bank is providing technical assistance to the Energy Regulatory Commission (ERC) to develop a baseline and provide recommendations for the country's first offshore wind regulatory framework, including tariff-setting, potential revenue support mechanisms and least-cost grid integration (ADB, 2022[8]).
- The Energy Transition Partnership (ETP) is also supporting the ERC to upgrade overall energy regulations (including the Philippines Grid Code) to accommodate modern renewable energy technologies, including offshore wind (ETP UNOPS, 2021[9]).
- Furthermore, Carbon Trust is supporting the DOE and other government agencies with two ongoing projects in the country. The first one is on Marine Spatial Planning (MSP) and will focus on creating the tools for a future MSP exercise led by the DOE, which would subsequently feed into the designation of offshore wind development zones in the country. The second one is on project permitting and consenting procedures. Both projects are currently at early stages of development and are expected to deliver over a timeline of 12-18 months. To facilitate the implementation of both projects, Carbon Trust has established the Philippine Offshore Wind – Joint Industry Platform (POWJIP), a forum to facilitate research, technical support, capacity building, and overall co-ordination between public and private stakeholders. It currently has 17 participants (including the DOE) and is funded by the Energy Transition Council's Rapid Response Facility.

Source: (OECD, 2022[8])

Offshore wind challenges and market development barriers

Building and operating offshore wind farms comes with a different set of challenges compared to other infrastructure projects. These include the inherent complexities of installing heavy structures in marine environments, as well as the integration of a highly diverse supply chain, which brings together a unique configuration of industrial sectors necessitating multiple interfaces with each other. The scale of operations needed to build an offshore wind farm requires carefully co-ordinated planning, project and risk management (Guillet, 2022[9]).

Figure 2.1. Offshore wind supply chain and key sectors

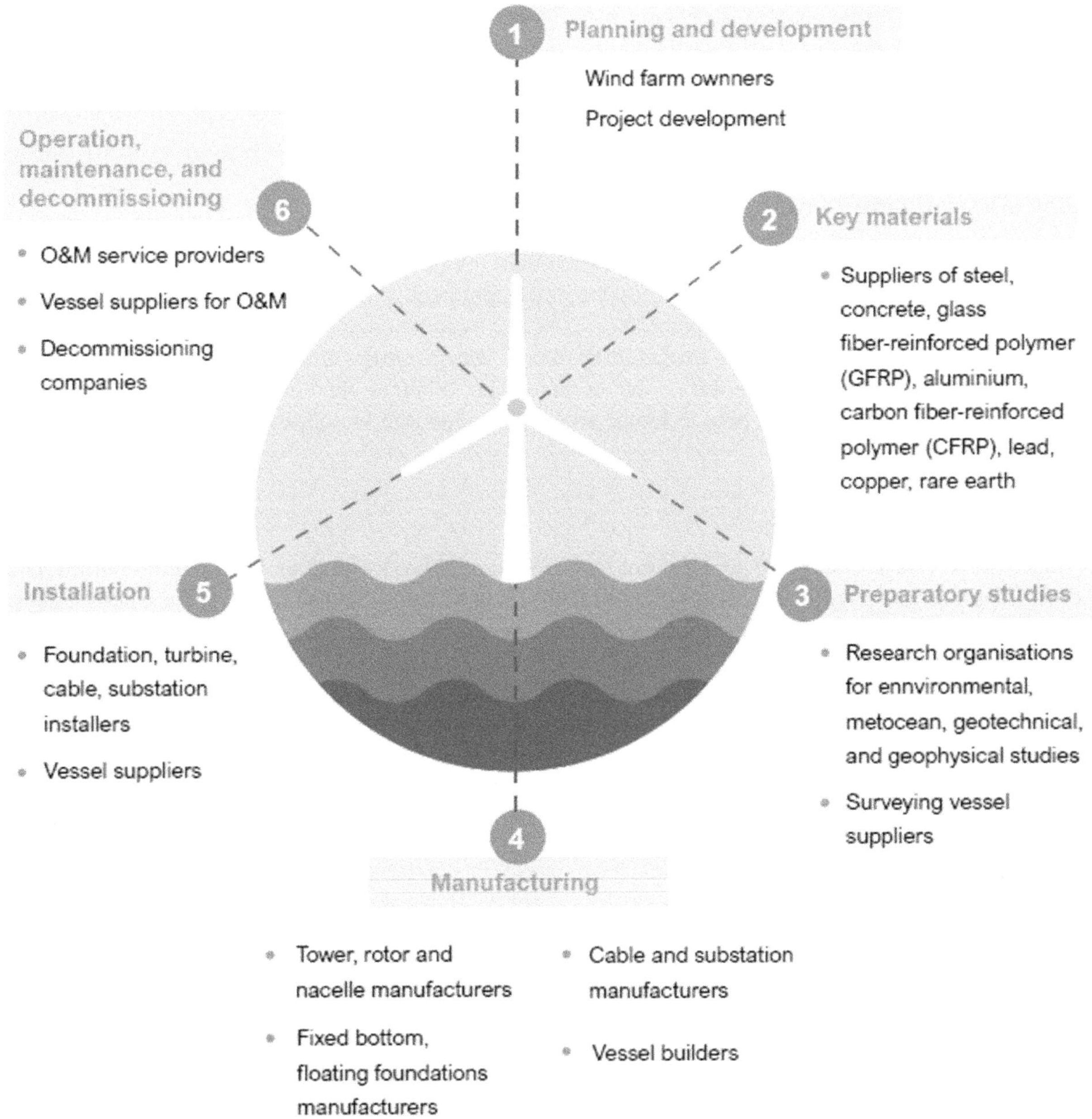

Source: Rabobank, 2023

Financing will play a key role in meeting offshore wind ambitions in the Philippines. The cost of capital is one of the largest determinants in the cost of electricity for offshore wind farms. It reflects the confidence investors and lenders have in achieving a return on their investment or debt respectively (IEA, 2022[10]). In OECD stakeholder consultations, developers indicated that for certain projects a 1% change in the cost of capital could lead to an 8% change in the cost of electricity. The nature of projects, with very high upfront costs and relatively low operational costs means that the cost of electricity will be driven predominantly by the cost of the repayment of the initial investment (in the form of dividends, debt repayments or both).

Individual GW-scale projects typically require around USD 2-3 billion of capital expenditure each and the first few projects usually experience the highest costs per GW generated (BVG Associates, n.d.[11]). However, gradual developments in infrastructure, local supply chains, and manufacturing capacities will bring economies of scale, create a pipeline of projects, and eventually lower the cost of energy from offshore wind. In the meantime, both real and perceived risks and barriers across the offshore wind value chain will need to be addressed to facilitate investments. This is even more important in the financing of the early projects, which have a crucial role in demonstrating the fundamentals of deploying offshore wind in the Philippines.

Policy and regulatory risk

Policy and regulations are critical to the development of offshore wind, as with many large-scale infrastructure projects. In many emerging markets, the economics of offshore wind can be challenging on a purely commercial basis (Shliomenzon, 2022[12]). As a proven technology being adopted in an emerging market, the regulatory framework is expected to evolve with experience. During this process, an open dialogue between government agencies, local communities, offshore wind developers and other players from the marine ecosystem, can help to better shape the rules that enable the formation of new market structures.

Offshore wind targets and consideration in the 2030 and 2040 power generation mix

Investors noted a lack of coherence, frequent revisions and different timelines between the current plans of different government agencies covering generation, transmission and distribution. This makes it difficult for developers to set realistic expectations on deployment volumes. The main provisions related to renewable energy and the power sector in the Philippines are contained in several plans covering power generation, renewable energy, and transmission at central and local government level. These are the **Philippine Energy Plan** (PEP), the **Power Development Plan** (PDP), the **National Renewable Energy Program** (NREP), and the **Transmission Development Plan** (TDP). The country's offshore wind potential is expected to be added in future editions of these plans, which are currently under discussion (as of September 2023). This provides an opportunity to harmonise these plans, including targets and revision horizons.

Offshore wind stable and predictable regulatory framework

The renewable energy sector in the Philippines presents an evolving nature to reflect industry, technological and cost developments. For offshore wind, a regulatory framework that will create the industry's operational model is still to be developed.

Under the current guidelines, wind energy service contracts (WESCs) are awarded on a first come, first-serve basis to any qualified developer proposing a project in a location that does not overlap with existing military, shipping, trade, or commercial zones. While the existing procedure has enabled many developers to secure WESCs quickly and commence pre-development activities, they don't provide a route to market.

During OECD stakeholder consultations, investors welcomed the launch of the systematic auction system for renewable energy capacity since 2022. They recognise it as an efficient model to award the most competitive renewable energy projects at the most competitive price, creating similar expectations for the offshore wind sector (see Table 2.3). The auction schedule is published annually, including technology installation targets per region for the upcoming three years (DOE, 2023[13]). Offshore wind is expected to be included in the 2024 GEAP auction round, but details on pricing, delivery schedules and other auction features are yet to be defined.

Risks related to planning, consenting and approvals

Slow planning and permitting can create significant delays, lock projects in lengthy development phases and slow down the market. Experience from more established markets shows that slow permitting has been a barrier in many parts of the world, including Europe, where over 80 GW of wind energy projects were stuck in permitting procedures in 2022 (Dixson-Declève, 2022[14]). During OECD stakeholder consultations in the Philippines, investors identified three key challenges during the planning and permitting phase. These include the site selection, reliable wind measurements and grid connection permit delays.

Environmental compliance certificates for LiDAR equipment

The rules and procedures currently applicable to offshore wind are derived from existing ones for onshore wind or offshore oil and gas projects (DOE, 2022[3]), and thus often fail to account for the specificities of offshore wind projects and create unnecessary hurdles for their development. Under these rules, developers require a certificate prior to the installation of the equipment for Light Detection and Ranging (LiDAR) mapping activities, which is needed to collect site-specific wind speed data as part of their WESC commitments. However, as LiDAR installations do not require drilling in the seabed, such a project should not have to go through an extensive and time-consuming permitting procedure, which in turn delays data collection and eventual deployment (OECD, 2022[15]).

Box 2.3. Obtaining a Wind Energy Service Contract (WESC) in the Philippines under the current guidelines

In the current set-up, developers are responsible for site selection, investigation and permitting. The wind energy service contract (WESC) is the license that enables developers in the Philippines to exclusively carry out preliminary investigations, construction and turbine installation, and exploitation of the wind resources for a specified number of years.

The current Philippine WESC format covers a 25-year timeframe, comprising five years of pre-development stage (e.g. securing permits, conducting feasibility studies, financial close and declaration of commerciality), five years of development stage (e.g. construction and commissioning) and the remainder for the commercial or operational phase. The WESC license is renewable once. DOE reserves the right to end the WESC contract if there is no progress in meeting the workplan milestones that developers have submitted, or if developers declare that their site is not technically and commercially feasible.

Developers first send a Letter of Intent (LOI) to the DOE proposing an indicative power capacity, deployment schedule and location for the project. The DOE then conducts a mapping verification procedure to confirm that the proposed location is available. If so, the developer is asked to register on EVOSS and submit legal, technical, and financial documents through the online portal to secure a preliminary business permit.

Once the permit is secured, the DOE is required to approve the project and award a WESC within 31 days; if not, the project is considered automatically approved under the rule of positive silence.

Source: Authors compilations from DOE resources and stakeholder consultations.

Wind measurements and reliable site-specific data

During OECD consultation workshops, developers indicated that the 5-year period currently allocated under the WESC framework for reliable wind measurements may not be sufficient to accomplish this and may need to be revised. Existing data for resource potential is limited to desk-based modelling, which is subject to a margin of error given the inconsistent and variable wind patterns in the Philippines (OECD, 2022[15]). The lack of reliable and site-specific data across technical, spatial, economic, environmental and social indicators for developers to optimally locate their offshore wind projects may also lead to delays in securing a WESC contract.

Grid system impact studies and grid connection permits

Development timelines on transmission infrastructure are also not representative of offshore wind and can delay the project financing. Developers noted that it can take up to 18 months in the early development stage for the NGCP to conduct a system impact study, which is needed to assess the project's viability in relation to the current grid (OECD, 2022[15]). Following the study, the NGCP communicates any changes or necessary upgrades to the DOE (NGCP, 2022[16]). Auctioned projects are granted a grid connection permit only after securing a power supply agreement (PSA) (World Bank, 2022[2]). Merchant projects, or those selling directly in the wholesale electricity spot market, do not need a PSA to obtain a grid connection permit. In either case, and from a lenders' perspective, no financing activities can start before any power supply agreements (public or corporate) and grid connection permits are in place, leading to interface risk.

Figure 2.2. Offshore wind development cycle

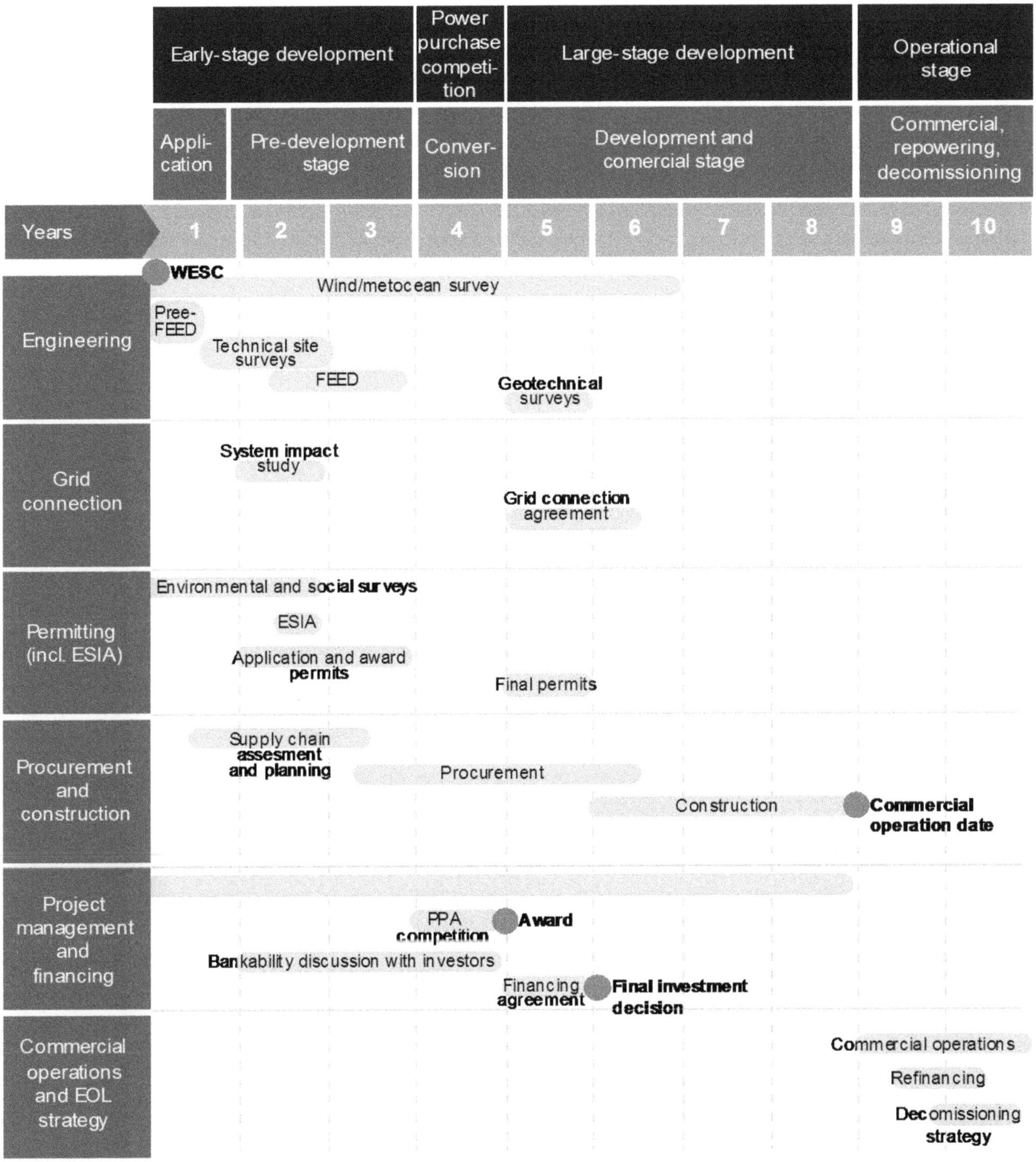

Source: Adapted from World Bank, 2022

Delays and costs linked to transmission infrastructure

Delays linked to transmission infrastructure

Even after access to the high voltage grid is secured in the permitting phase, grid connection delays can happen at any point before and during construction. This can result in project commissioning delays and most likely budget overruns (Guillet, 2022[9]). Developers in the Philippines face long connection delays. Some of the awarded capacity under the FIT system in 2016 did not get connected fully until 2021.

The latest Transmission Development Plan (TDP) 2022-2040, includes plans to upgrade and expand the transmission network to accommodate offshore wind power plants proposed under awarded WESCs (NGCP, 2022[16]). However, stakeholders noted that transmission infrastructure upgrades can take up to 10 years in needs assessments, planning, designing and implementation, as the process often encounters political, administrative and capacity related challenges (OECD, 2022[15]).

Although the DOE is involved in endorsement of power projects and approval of the final transmission development plan, the choice of priority projects and the corresponding timelines for construction ultimately rests with the NGCP. The legal auction framework of 2022 mainly allocated grid reliability responsibilities to the transmission and distribution network providers, which must conduct system tests to allow commercial operation of awarded projects. Any needed adjustments resulting from the system impact studies should be communicated to the DOE to avoid system problems and delays in connection (IRENA, 2022[17]).

Costs and financing of point-to-point transmission lines

Section 9 of EPIRA (RA 9136) allows developers and generation companies to build, own and operate their own project transmission lines. While the system impact study and the grid related permits rest primarily with the NGCP, the construction of transmission facilities can be considered part of the generating asset.

Under current asset boundary classifications, developers may be required to finance any point-to-point transmission lines that have been endorsed by the DOE and NGCP and subsequently included in the transmission development plan (TDP). This is the case provided such facilities are not shared by other generation power plants. Developers may also be responsible for the operation and maintenance, as well as any needed upgrades. For offshore wind this would include the cost of financing and operating subsea transmission lines, offshore substations and connections to mainland.

Should any of these transmission facilities be required for competitive purposes to be used by other power plants, the asset ownership will be transferred to TransCo at a fair market price. Any disagreement on the transfer will be settled by the Energy Regulatory Committee (ERC), who will also determine the fair market value of the asset.

Such a set-up comes with certain advantages. At project level, internalising the transmission build-out in the project construction schedule presents less risk of construction delays. It also allows a developer to use the same substation to connect their other offshore wind farms within the same zone and bring down costs for consecutive offshore wind farms.

However, at regional or national level, such project-by-project approach could potentially lead to unco-ordinated onshore grid upgrades by the grid operator, and duplication of work and resources. The lack of a proactive grid planning risks resulting in higher costs for both developers and the grid operator.

Supply chain and technology risk

Rising costs in the offshore wind supply chain

The complexity and scale of the offshore wind supply chain is reflected in the set of industrial sectors that it brings together. This includes the wind farm owners and operators, the developers, suppliers of key raw materials, the equipment manufacturers, the construction and installation of turbines at sea (including vessel suppliers), the financiers and legal advisers and the operation and maintenance service providers (see Figure 2.1).

In the Philippines, the offshore wind sector will need to rely extensively on imports of key components at least in the early days (World Bank, 2022[1]), which may present some bottlenecks and delays, as well as geopolitical dependency. Also, given the increased interest in offshore wind from other regional markets such as Viet Nam, Japan and South Korea, developers in the Philippines may have to compete for components, logistical vessels, skills, capital and other resources while the domestic supply chain gradually builds up over time.

Moreover, offshore wind is also exposed to other commodity risk given its reliance on raw materials such as steel, iron and copper (Janipour, 2023[18]). Inflation has resulted in higher material and logistical costs that impact the capital expenditure required and eventually project viability. It is for this reason that cost reductions in wind energy in European and US markets have been partly offset by higher turbine prices (+40% up in the last two years) and supply chain disruptions.

Figure 2.3. Evolution of wind energy turbine prices

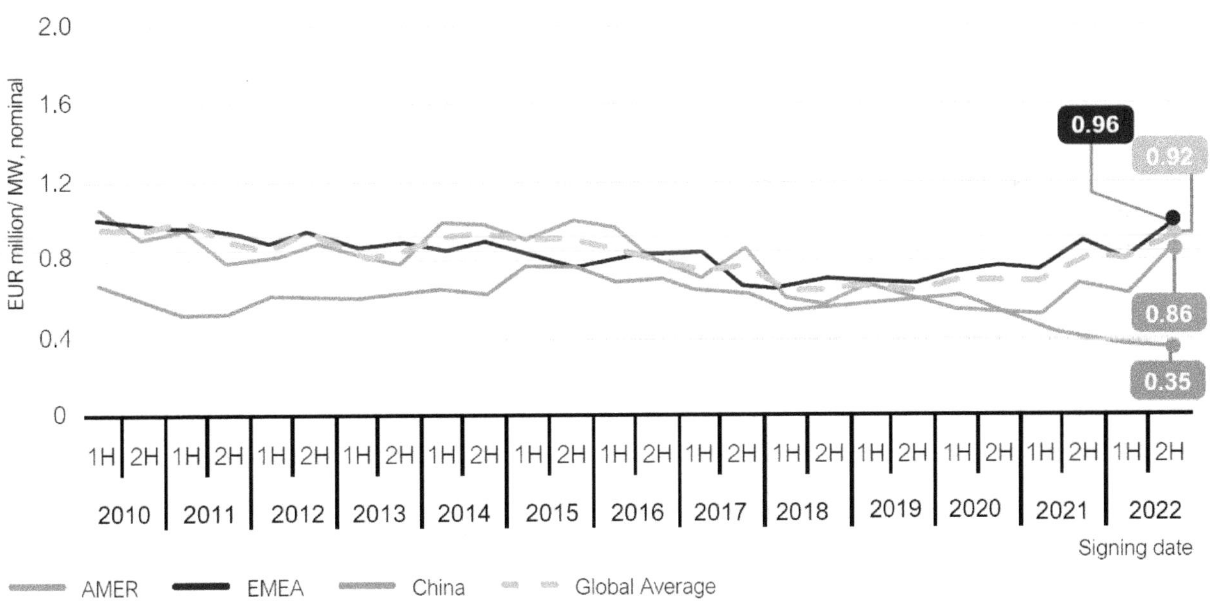

Source: Rabobank and BloombergNEF, 2023

All these developments suggest the Philippines may be relying on regional supply chains, mostly in Asia, dominated by Chinese turbine manufacturers. While cost management is important, security of supply and quality control are equally crucial in delivering a timely project. Any potential delays will require higher contingency budgets from the financiers.

Turbine technology and extreme wind speeds

Although the first few projects in the Philippines will rely on commercially mature fixed-bottom technology, the extreme wind resource conditions in the country could pose a significant challenge for construction and turbine installation and encourage instead the use of floating technology. Extreme weather patterns could also be a concern during transportation, storage and the operational lifetime of an offshore wind farm. Any risk of potential damage to physical assets will be reflected in the risk premia of insurance contracts, which is a requirement by most lenders. In natural catastrophe (NAT CAT) exposed areas, the cost of ensuring offshore wind can be significantly higher than non-exposed areas. This can vary from 0.3% to 3%, depending on the phase of a project lifecycle (construction, operation) and project track record (NARDAC, 2023[19]).

Current offshore wind turbines can withstand wind speeds of up to 70m/s, whereas in the Philippines, wind speeds of over 100 m/s can be seen in the north and east of the country (World Bank, 2022[1]). Technological advancements in the global offshore wind industry could help mitigate the risk of extreme weather events. The current turbine technology is already prepared to some extent for higher wind speeds, as typhoon-grade turbines are becoming available in the market.

Further, as 90% of the offshore wind resource potential in the Philippines is concentrated in deep waters, sustained growth will rely on floating technology (World Bank, 2022[2]). As floating offshore wind takes off from demonstration and small-scale projects to multi-turbine commercial arrays by 2030, the technology is also expected to reach global cost competitiveness (Fitch Solutions, 2022[20]). The Philippines could in fact become a regional leader by demonstrating early floating offshore wind projects and developing local manufacturing capacity for their components, thereby accelerating cost reductions.

Merchant risk and counterparty risk

Merchant risk

Merchant risk is the full exposure of a project to short-term electricity prices, thereby creating uncertainties on both price and volume. In the Philippines, most of the renewable energy power sources are exposed to some degree of market risk following the FIT phase-out.

Long-term power purchase agreements (PPAs) can partly mitigate some of the merchant exposure by guaranteeing a minimum price on the volumes sold. The current auction framework allocates contracts based on 20-year power supply agreements with the government, paid in accordance with actual electricity generated as per wholesale electricity spot market rules. A ceiling price (GEAR) is disclosed by the DOE prior to the auction. Contracts are awarded based on minimum price bids called Green Energy Tariffs (GET) until the demand band for a specific technology is met. (DOE, 2021[21]). The 20-year contract duration is considered to provide sufficient tariff certainty for a project to repay the lenders.

Long term PPAs partially limit a project's exposure to price risk, but uncertainty on the volume of sales remains entirely with the asset owners. Variability of weather patterns may have an impact on power generation and lead to a mismatch between what is produced and what is sold. Too much production can be curtailed, while too little production can lead to lower than anticipated project revenues. Fluctuations on project revenues increases the risk of access to finance and raises questions on a project's capability to service debt (IEA, 2022[10]).

Lenders are familiar with merchant risk financing, predominantly from oil and gas sector financing. During OECD stakeholder consultations, some of the largest Philippine banks indicated they have assumed some merchant risk financing even in renewable energy projects for onshore wind and solar in the post-FIT phase. High energy prices, sector maturity, shorter construction schedules and falling costs for both onshore wind and solar have made this possible. Developers enter short-term loans with commercial banks (as opposed to long term loans, which need long-term price stability), with a view to then refinance should the electricity prices change.

However, this is not the case for offshore wind farms where capital expenditure is significantly higher, development schedules are longer, construction at sea is riskier and the project track record is not there yet. Spot market prices are too volatile to provide a basis for long-term, capital intensive and price-taking infrastructure projects. The capacity of the smallest offshore wind WESC awarded is 10 times higher than the average renewable energy project currently in operation in the Philippines. Moreover, in project finance transactions, all syndicate banks would have to go on equal terms. Depending on their profile and capitalisation, not all banks may be willing to accept merchant risk elements in project finance.

Counterparty risk

Even when a long-term PPA agreement is secured, there is still counterparty risk that needs to be addressed. A highly concentrated market structure amongst the distribution utilities has resulted in a limited pool of creditworthy off-takers and raises questions on the country's future capacity to purchase utility scale offshore wind production (World Bank, 2022[1]). Meralco - the Philippines largest utility dominant in the Luzon region, and VECO - the second largest utility in the Philippines dominant in the Visayas region, together own 76% of the total consumption in the country (WESM, 2023[22]). This is further compounded by the Philippine regional context and the different demand and supply profiles of each of the three main grids (see Box 1.1).

Moreover, the market for corporate off-takers and non-utility PPAs remains limited, despite the Philippines having enacted measures to enable the market such as the Green Energy Option Programme (GEOP) and the Retail Competition and Open Access (RCOA). Investors have highlighted low confidence in such practices as the sector has been fraught with low compliance and in some cases, unilateral termination of contracts for contestable consumers.[1] In 2022, the ERC had received over 16 complaints linked to disconnection claims from large industry players, together representing over 126 MW capacity impacted (ERC, 2022[23]).

Setting the course for an offshore wind market in the Philippines

Capital expenditure for offshore wind projects in the Philippines could reach USD 50 billion by 2040 (World Bank, 2022[1]). Meanwhile, in the last decade the Philippines has only financed renewable energy projects at an average rate of USD 900 million per year. With investment requirements increasing from millions to billions, the question of capital availability becomes critical to enabling the Philippine renewable energy industry, notably, for offshore wind.

The offshore wind risks outlined above fall under three main categories: political and regulatory risks, sector specific risks and offshore wind project specific risks. What these risks mean for the lenders and equity investors, and how well they're managed and absorbed in financial structures, will determine the availability and cost of capital for offshore wind in the Philippines.

Central to all this is a stable regulatory framework, strong market fundamentals and investment predictability, including for local supporting infrastructure. A stakeholder poll conducted at the 2nd OECD-DOE Clean Energy Finance and Investment workshop found that 71% of the participants viewed a simplified regulatory framework as the key immediate priority for initial offshore wind development in the Philippines, followed by transmission infrastructure (19%) and designating offshore wind development zones (10%).

Long-term vision and strategy

A clear role for fixed and floating offshore wind in the country's power development plans

To encourage the market to set the right expectations on future volumes, a specific role for both fixed and floating offshore wind can be considered in the 2030, 2040 and 2050 power generation mix. Having separate targets for both technologies will enable the industry to run accurate cost and revenue estimates, set cost reduction pathways via economies of scale and optimise industry learning curves. Having a long-term vision also lays the groundwork for developing a domestic supply chain in the country, enabling infrastructure, manufacturing capabilities and the skill set needed to implement utility scale offshore wind with higher local content.

Coherent and co-ordinated strategic development plans

Given the scale and complexity of the offshore wind supply chain, enhanced cross-government collaboration is needed to convert the high offshore wind potential into bankable projects. Offshore wind is entirely new to the country. As such, the current state of development plans in the Philippines reflects an evolving but fragmented nature at central and local government level.

In the announced whole-of-government approach, a better alignment can be sought between different but interlinked sectors such as maritime planning, power generation, transmission and distribution – all of which are currently treated in separate development plans subject to different revision horizons. This will ensure that climate and energy policies are coherent, calibrated against each other and re-aligned with the high offshore wind potential of the Philippines. This can be reflected in co-ordinated Maritime Spatial Planning, Power Development Plans, National Renewable Energy Plans, and Transmission Development Plans.

Onshore support facilities as a key market enabler

Offshore wind farms typically involve a combination of components that are assembled on land, and others at sea. As such, onshore support facilities, mostly to strengthen and modernise port infrastructure, will also require significant investments for the Philippines to realise its offshore wind potential (both fixed and floating) and reach economies of scale. In the medium term, this includes adequate transportation and port terminals, storage and assembly point for components, training areas, as well as dedicated areas related to operation and maintenance facilities. In the longer term, this can include hosting the needed infrastructure for floating offshore wind and for converting offshore wind power into renewable hydrogen. Currently, there is no single port or industrial site in the Philippines that can deliver the full range of services to build large scale offshore wind projects.

Strong collaboration between central government, local government and the different agencies involved in offshore wind planning is key to bringing the needed infrastructure upgrades for the designated Philippine offshore wind ports. The Department of Energy (DOE) has already started consultations with the Philippine Port Authority (PPA), the Department of Transport (DOT) and the National Grid Corporation of the Philippines (NGCP). Nine priority ports have been identified and the government is looking into business models for financing ports and related onshore infrastructure.

To facilitate finance and investments, the Government can consider a multiport strategy, where different ports collaborate to provide different services during different stages of a project lifecycle. This is particularly important for floating offshore wind, which has the highest technical potential in the Philippines. One of the biggest challenges for floating offshore wind will be the scale of port infrastructure needed in relation to the economic activity in the surrounding areas and the normal business operations of ports outside of offshore wind. As such, it is important that the readiness assessment of the potential offshore wind ports balances expectations of redevelopment and economic feasibility.

Given the strategic nature of ports, these investments can be funded with a combination of public and private capital. Investments in ports have a relatively short payback period, estimated at five years (WindEurope, 2021[24]). This makes ports related infrastructure an interesting investment opportunity for the private sector. Aspiring floating offshore wind markets are looking at models and initiatives that bring together port authorities and wind energy developers to pull out the resources needed for strategic investments. Three different phases for developer collaboration can be identified (Reuters, 2023[25]):

a. The initial port assessment where developers can share the cost of assessing the necessary port upgrades (estimated at USD 50 000 – 100 000).

b. Elaboration of the port development plan, where developers can share the cost as future users (estimated at USD 3 – 4 million).

c. To a lesser extent, port upgrades and major works can also be considered for collaboration. However, different developer requirements, technology specifications and competition concerns make co-operation challenging in the actual investment phase.

In the Philippines, the port infrastructure readiness assessment is expected to be funded by the Asian Development Bank, whereas the actual investments in the ports will be the responsibility of port owners. The revision of the Build-Operate-Transfer (BOT) law in the Philippines in 2022, provides an opportunity to bring more equity investments in ports by speeding up the process of establishing viable Public Private Partnership (PPP) models for public infrastructure. The revised BOT law also reflects a more appropriate risk allocation between the public and private sector, which improves the PPP bankability.

Concessional finance from multilateral development banks can also play an important role in bridging the investment gap needed for the upgrade of ports and onshore support facilities. Long term investments can pose challenges to ports, which normally finance their operations on working capital and revolving loans. As such, it is important to combine development finance with the current credit facilities in use.

To facilitate lending from banks, investment certainty and project pipeline will be key to raising the needed financing. As with other long-term investments, lenders would typically require revenue certainty for port upgrades to cover the debt service throughout the duration of the loan. This can be in the form of estimated utilisation rates and contracts. This investment certainty can only be secured with a frontloaded auction schedule, supported by timely planning and permitting, and facilitated by the allocation of specific offshore wind development zone areas.

Planning and permitting

Creating an offshore wind one-stop shop

One-stop shops and the creation of a unified permitting authority can simplify early project development by avoiding the risk of duplication and reducing administrative barriers to entry. Some departments, like the Department of Environment and Natural Resources (DENR) and the Department of Energy (DOE), have already started to review and customise their respective regulations and processes to include the specific characteristics of offshore wind. However, a more extensive review process would benefit all government agencies involved in approving offshore wind projects. Moreover, this should also be extended to permitting of supporting activities in the supply chain (e.g. the opening of factories).

The permit granting process comes with many different decisions from many different agencies. The DOE's Executive Order, approved by the President in April 2023, will create an Offshore Wind Development and Investment Council comprising 10 government agencies. The council will aim to encourage the review, to update and streamline permitting and approval procedures in accordance with Good International Industry Practices (GIIP). This effectively means the creation of a custom one-stop shop for offshore wind projects, to be eventually integrated into the EVOSS system (Mercurio, 2022[26]).

To boost the efficacy of one-stop shop solutions, further measures will be needed.

- Investing in human and digital resources for the offshore wind one-stop shop will ensure the process is efficient, transparent and consistent.
- The industry expects clear decision timelines on permit applications, maintaining consistent permitting requirements across agencies, ensuring durability and exclusive permits once awarded, and facilitating co-ordination among public agencies and private stakeholders.
- Political commitment, role-clarity and governance issues within the one-stop shop will need to be addressed early on to avoid any operationalisation delays.
- Finally, the Philippines already applies "positive silence" in the WESC award process. Maintaining the same practice would benefit the offshore wind one-stop shop concept.

Reliable site-specific data to allocate special zone areas

Designating specific areas for development can speed up a lengthy planning and permitting phase for projects. In the short-term, the Government needs data and information on site selection to facilitate the allocation of special zone areas. To deploy offshore wind safely and rapidly, developers require reliable and site-specific data across technical, spatial, economic, environmental, social and infrastructural indicators. Bathymetric and geological data collected as part of past offshore oil and gas field projects provide a good starting point for developers seeking site-specific technical data. Other relevant topographical data – for instance, exposure to earthquakes or typhoon risks – can already be found on the National Mapping and Resource Information Authority (NAMRIA) public database.

Non-technical data collection is equally important to ensure that offshore wind projects are located in low-risk areas. Robust spatial mapping of marine ecosystems and endangered species and surveys of local fishing communities operating in high resource potential areas are required to avoid any potential conflicts linked to high environmental and social risks. A detailed mapping of military zones and shipping routes, available port and shipyard infrastructure, and access to regional supply chains would also be crucial in identifying optimal plant locations and determining infrastructure investment needs. Some of these data can be collected and published as part of a future government-led MSP exercise.

Further, site-specific measurements of wind speeds and patterns, which need to be conducted by developers, are subject to additional permits adopted from the oil and gas sector that are not applicable to offshore wind. This adds further delays in data collection. DENR is currently revising the procedures for obtaining permission to install LiDAR equipment.

The existing datasets are currently housed within different government departments. This would need to be consolidated and made publicly available to improve transparency and efficiency. In the medium term, the DOE can foresee a unified data room under its supervision that can serve as a repository of the different datasets, as well as related legislation that is essential for planning, permitting and developing an offshore wind project. In the longer term, the data platform can take a broader scope including other renewable energy sources that can support the identification of specific renewable go-to areas, similar to EU emergency measures that were enacted in 2021 to cope with the energy crisis (JRC, 2022[27]). Such tools can be integrated in the one-stop shop procedures and help national and regional authorities plan key infrastructure, including transmission grids, roads and ports.

Ongoing technical assistances from the Energy Transition Partnership, the Carbon Trust and the World Bank on energy regulations, maritime spatial planning and grid related standards, will help identify concrete actions to accelerate permitting for offshore wind. They should provide a comprehensive review of the three main offshore wind challenges for projects in development phase: administrative approval process, site selection and grid connection.

Grid connection planning and development

Grid connection permits and development zones

Significant responsibility for project selection rests with the grid operator NGCP. Reforming the procedure for selecting projects for inclusion in the TDP and ensuring the DOE is more closely involved in this process can help ensure transmission assets get built in tandem with offshore wind projects.

The allocation of special zone areas can also help co-ordinate the effort and investments needed for upgrading the onshore grid facilities. This approach facilitates the optimisation of space and resources, while reducing the risk of connection delays. The World Bank is conducting a modelling and systems planning exercise to identify priority locations for grid development as part of its current technical assistance to the DOE. The results from this activity can help the DOE identify specific transmission needs of offshore wind and potentially fast-track certain priority transmission projects for inclusion in the TDP.

This would allow the DOE to side-step the typically long process of endorsements and system impact studies and create a faster avenue for priority transmission projects to get built. Similarly, integrating offshore wind into the Competitive Renewable Energy Zones (CREZ) would also help accelerate corresponding transmission projects to be included in the TDP.

Finance and ownership of the transmission line

The current asset boundary classifications under the grid code would need to be further clarified and a transparent recovery mechanism for ownership transfer of transmission lines would need to be in place. While the system impact study is the responsibility of NGCP, the construction of transmission lines to the shore would typically be considered part of the generation asset and is therefore the responsibility of the developer. However, once the offshore network is developed, it can create positive externalities for other projects and the grid system more broadly. The current legal basis provides a recovery mechanism for such assets, whose ownership will be transferred to TransCo. Given the high transmission costs of building and operating the connection to shore, a transparent methodology for allocating the fair market price can be made publicly available to investors. This can also include provisions for the operation and maintenance of transmission lines after the decommissioning of the wind farm once the project reaches its end of life.

Financing innovation in grid infrastructure

Smart grids are critical to the deployment of renewable energy at scale (IEA, 2022[28]). Nonetheless, there is little consideration for this topic in the transmission development plan of the NGCP. Alongside financing grid expansion and upgrade, both transmission and distribution operators should also focus on financing innovation in grid infrastructure. In a fragmented network like the Philippines, grid optimisation based on digital technologies can play a critical role to reduce congestion issues and loss of revenues for the generators resulting from curtailment measures (IEA, 2022[28]).

Offshore wind regulatory framework

Competitive procurement for projects in the Green Energy Auction Program

A competitive procurement mechanism for offshore wind projects can ensure transparency, efficiency and certainty regarding future offshore wind development in the Philippines. The currently awarded offshore wind WESCs have enabled developers to start with exploration, development and feasibility studies. The Green Energy Auction Program (GEAP) could provide a framework for competitive procurement for offshore wind projects.

Alongside auctions, the government can maintain an "open door policy" for developer led offshore wind deployment, provided the projects obtain all the necessary technical, environmental and grid connection permits to allow them access to the wholesale electricity spot market.

Adequate visibility on timing, technologies, and volumes

The government announcement for systematic auctions is a welcome development. The industry expects offshore wind to be integrated in the upcoming rounds of GEAP auctions with clear, upfront visibility for two to three years. Regular auctions are important to sustain cost reductions, ensure fair competition, and provide a sense of timing to the industry and the supply chain. Decisions to invest in supporting infrastructure (ports, factories, test facilities, logistics) and skills development rely on a predictable project pipeline that can only be secured with a near- and medium-term visibility on auctions.

Alongside frequent and predictable auctions, developers also expect technology-specific demand bands. This will avoid offshore wind competing with other more mature technologies while ensuring a diversified power generation mix in each of the three main regions, with a wide range of complementary technologies.

Consideration for non-price criteria in auctions

Non-price criteria can be integrated in auction design, provided measurable and unambiguous performance indicators are in place, and provided they don't create additional administrative burden on the projects or duplicate existing permits and measures. Several policy regimes in other offshore wind markets are also looking at broader sustainability considerations.

In the medium term, the Philippines too can consider including sustainability criteria in the current legal auction framework. This can help mitigate some of the environmental and social risks related to biodiversity, and, in the long-term, lead to more local content in the supply chain, particularly in manufacturing capacity.

Non-price criteria can also promote innovation. The latter is important should the DOE allow co-located technologies to compete in auctions. Co-located technologies can include generating assets with storage, electrolysers, or even a combination of offshore wind and floating solar. This can facilitate the integration of renewables to the grid, address some of the grid congestion challenges and risk of curtailment and improve the capacity factor and economics of the generating asset. New business models of co-located technologies are emerging in major offshore wind markets (Jansen et al., 2022[29]) (Lee, 2023[30]). Designing the auction system to keep it open for further integration of other renewable power generation will lower the risk of lock-in situations.

Addressing merchant risk in offshore wind projects in the Philippines

Auction design and revenue regime

The early offshore wind projects in the Philippines will need some form of revenue stabilisation, granted through competitive auctions, to be economically viable. This is especially the case for floating offshore wind, which in the Philippines is most of the sites. But it is also important for the early fixed-bottom offshore wind projects. Whilst the technology is proven, its application in the Philippines is new and this will be priced in the cost of capital. According to international practice from offshore wind auctions, early wind farms and emerging markets tend to rely on fixed price revenue regimes, either through FiTs or through PPAs.

The current auctions in the Philippines award a 20-year-long power supply agreements with a fixed price regime. A ceiling price is set by the ERC and developers bid for a strike price until the maximum volume per technology is fulfilled. This is comparable and aligned with the auction design in some of the major offshore wind markets in Europe. Nonetheless, some areas for improvement that were highlighted in the 2nd OECD-DOE Clean Energy Finance and Investment workshop are as follows:

- A transparent costing methodology needs to be developed for offshore wind prior to establishing the ceiling prices (GEAR). This costing methodology will need to reflect evolving market prices while appropriately balancing the value of offshore wind (e.g. power system services, alternative uses like in green hydrogen production, etc.) against the levelised cost of electricity estimates.
- To mitigate some of the macro-economic risks in a project, it is important to index to inflation the tariffs granted under the auction programme. This will preserve the revenue stability of the offshore wind supply chain, investor confidence in the sector and consequently the jobs and economic value added that offshore wind projects bring. This is also aligned with recent initiatives from established offshore wind markets.

A well-designed revenue regime should aim to minimise risk for investors, while limiting the impact on public finances. The most effective mechanisms are the ones granted through competitive auctions and providing price visibility over 15-20 years. The longer the duration of the revenue regime, the easier it is for lenders and investors to amortise the financing costs over the years. This leads to lower financing costs and, in turn, lower electricity prices for consumers, as these are costs that will not be passed on (IEA, 2022[10]).

It is also important for any kind of public support to avoid the payment of extraordinary revenues. This would put into question the competitiveness of the technology and would come under scrutiny from the public, especially lenders, who are sceptical of over-remuneration. In five out of the eight largest offshore wind jurisdictions, contracts-for-difference (CfDs) have been used to provide price stability to investors (see Table 2.3) and protect consumers from high electricity prices (Florence School of Regulation, 2023[31]). A majority of these are two-sided CfDs, providing a minimum and maximum protection for the projects against volatile market prices. The two-way design means that projects also pay back when wholesale electricity prices are high, thereby guaranteeing the government and the consumers with low electricity prices.

Corporate PPAs as additional revenue streams

Alongside revenue stabilisation, corporate power purchase agreements (PPAs) can serve as an additional source of revenue for developers to access long term debt and command a lower cost of capital. Large industrial players who are heavy energy users can serve as creditworthy off-takers. In Europe and the US, corporate PPAs have been successfully implemented in utility scale projects, alongside policy support. As common practice, large corporate off-takers are bound by additionality principles when choosing the source of power, whereby they only engage in new renewable energy projects that wouldn't have otherwise reached the market.

Given the large offshore wind volumes to be procured, offshore wind regulatory frameworks need to allow large non-utility corporates to participate in a project alongside distribution utilities and policy support. In this way, project developers can be allowed to reserve a share of the generation for sale via PPA. The certificate-based tracking of procured power, available since mid-2022 with the launch of the Renewable Energy Market, should facilitate the uptake of such business models.

The Green Energy Option Programme, the Renewable Performance Standards and the Renewable Energy Market can provide the basis for a liquid and bankable corporate PPA market. However, confidence in these measures needs to be built. To achieve this, tools can be made available to structure flexible corporate PPA contracts that provide price visibility to the power generator and cost management to the off-taker in a two-sided contract for difference with a minimum and a maximum price. This can be supported further by clear and unambiguous terms on recourse in the event of payment default and a transparent dispute resolution mechanism in the event of contract breaches.

Table 2.2. Corporate PPAs secured alongside policy support for offshore wind projects

Project	Offtaker	Developer	Country	COD	PPA signed	Project (MW)	PPA (MW)	PPA tenor (Years)
Norther	Google	Engie	Belgium	2020	2019	370	92	5
Race bank	Nestle	Orsted	UK	2018	2020	573	31	15
Borkum Riffgrund 3	Covestro	Orsted	Germany	2025	2019	900	100	10
Race bank	NW	Orsted	UK	2018	2019	573	23	10
Borssele III&IV	Microsoft	Eneco, Shell	Netherlands	2021	2019	731	90	15
Nordsee Ost	Deutsche Bahn	Innogy, RWE	Germany	2015	2019	295	25	5

Source: Green Giraffe, 2020

Hedging against wind volume risk

While a minimum price can be guaranteed via PPA contracts, developers are still exposed to some volume risk, which results from deviations between wind estimates and actual production. In cases where wind variability is high, hedging products developed by insurance companies can create value in the energy commodity business. They can be structured as floor on power output. Hedging the wind risk can protect project revenues against unpredictable weather patterns and downside scenarios.

Certainty of demand for power and curtailment risk from insufficient grid capacity

To be able to raise low-cost finance, offshore wind projects in the Philippines would need to see a certainty of demand for power and the ability to deliver the power to where it is needed. Curtailment measures in the Philippines have been taken even for renewable energy projects that benefit from priority dispatch or policy support. Production based support schemes for renewables or PPA contracts such as in the Philippines will not be funded if the power is curtailed and will result in missed revenues for asset generators. Curtailment measures are also not subject to financial products that hedge against commodity risk, leaving projects fully exposed to downside scenarios.

Box 2.4. Comparison of existing auction mechanisms and prices in main offshore wind markets

Auctions have emerged as the instrument of choice for deploying offshore wind capacity globally. Over 53 offshore wind auctions have been conducted globally, the majority in Europe – which has the longest track record in offshore wind. Auctions are primarily used to competitively allocate support measures, which range from fixed tariffs to zero-subsidy. Each of the support measures currently in use (FITs, one-sided or two-sided CFDs, PPAs, Renewable Energy Certificates (RECs) will expose investors to different levels of market risks.

Early and less mature markets tend to use revenue stabilisation mechanisms more extensively and limit to a large scale the merchant risk exposure of developers. None of the offshore wind jurisdictions to date have chosen to expose investors to merchant risk in the early market stages. In the initial market stages in Europe, fixed price support served to incentivise investments through de-risking and enabled the continent to build track record.

In more established markets, developers need less de-risking. This can be seen in Europe, which is transitioning towards more market based and higher risk sharing support regimes. Some countries have even introduced zero subsidy tenders (the Netherlands) or allow negative bidding (Germany). This means two things: full merchant risk exposure in both cases and, in the latter, investors paying for the right to develop. Other countries like the UK have opted to reduce the risk for investors via two-sided CfD.

Stakeholder polling during OECD consultation workshops revealed that FiTs were considered the most effective fiscal support mechanism for initial offshore wind deployment in the Philippines (41% of the vote), followed by tax incentives (30%), contracts-for-difference (22%), feed-in premiums (4%) and tradeable certificates (4%).

Markets also differ in other auction design features such as: i) frequency of auctions; ii) duration of support; iii) market reference price; iv) adjustment for inflation; v) grid-connection responsibility; vi) site development responsibility; vii) allocation of seabed leases; and viii) penalty for non-compliance. Additional policy support outside of the revenue stabilisation mechanisms is granted in some markets, either in the form of development capital support or organised centrally by the government in specific offshore wind development zones. While each of these design features will have an impact on the final bid, awarded prices over the years have shown a significant reduction.

Figure 2.4. Average strike prices and offshore wind auctioned capacity in Europe

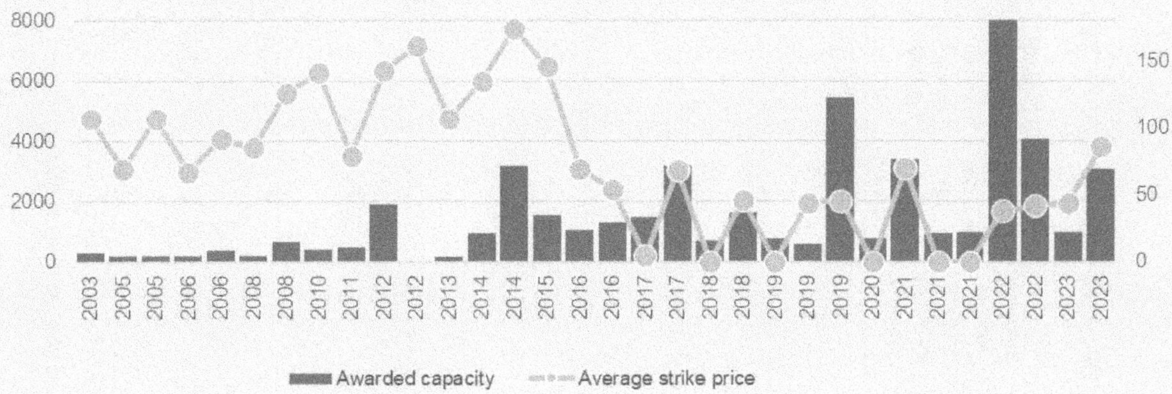

Source : WindEurope, 2023; Jansen et.al, 2022

StatLink https://stat.link/0pjq7k

Table 2.3. Overview of main fixed-bottom offshore wind auction design in established offshore wind markets (as of December 2021)

Country	Number of auctions (& auctioned projects)	Auctioned projects reaching FID (% of capacity)	Capacity weighted average prices (€2020/ MWh)	Funding mechanism (CfD, FIT, tax credit)	Tenor (years)	Inflation indexed	Grid connection responsibility	Site development	Seabed lease auction	Devex support	Penalties for non-compliance	Technology specific
China	7 (21)	9 (36.8%)	103.1	Administrative FIT/competitive FIT	n/a	No	Guaranteed access	n/a	n/a	n/a	Permit loss w/o construction >2 years	Yes
United Kingdom	4 (9)	8 (99.9%)	66.5	Two-sided CfD	15	Yes	Project	Bidder	Yes, separate auction prior CfD	No	Non-delivery: Banned for 2 years	Partial (different technology pots)
Germany	3 (13)	9 (54.2%)	15.1	One-sided CfD	20	No	TSO (socialised)	Government	No	Yes	Financial €0.1–0.2/MW	Yes
Netherlands	8 (8)	7 (83.2%)	26.8	One-sided CfD	15	No	TSO (socialised)	Government	Yes, part of auction criteria	Yes	Non-delivery: €10m Late: €3.5m/mo	Yes
Denmark	8 (8)	5 (83.8%)	89.4	Two-sided CfD	20	No	Project (as of 2021)	Bidder	No	No	Non-delivery/Late: =€m0.15/MW + less supported production	Yes
Chinese Taipei	2 (14)	6 (38.2%)	90.8	Administrative FIT/competitive FIT	20	No	TSO (socialised)	Government	No	No	No	Yes
United States	9 (13)	1 (9.4%)	75.5	Fixed OREC / fixed-priced PPA	20	Yes	Project	Bidder	Yes, prior federal seabed auctions	No	No	Yes
France	5 (8)	4 (42.0%)	133.7	FIT / two-sided CfD	20	Yes (for 60% of the tariff)	TSO (socialised)	Bidder	No	No	CfD shorted by the number of days delayed	Yes
Philippines (based on current GEAP)	na	na	na	Fixed price PPA	20	No	Project (to be further clarified)	Bidder	No	No	Delay >1 year: performance bond; Delay<1 year: 0.1%/day to a max of 10% of project cost	Partial (different technology bands)

Source: Adapted from Jansen et.al, 2022

Table 2.4. Overview of main policies in floating offshore wind policies (as of October 2023)

Main auction design elements	France	United Kingdom	Norway	Spain	Ireland	Italy	Portugal	Greece
Floating wind target	**Yes** 750 MW (3x250 MW) by 2030 and 1500 MW (extensions)	**Yes** 5000 MW by 2030	**Yes** 1500 MW	**Yes** 1000 - 3000 MW	**Partially** 5000 MW of mostly bottom fixed offshore wind by 2030, with strong potential afterwards	**Partially** 3500 MW of offshore wind without breakdown	**Yes** 2000 MW	**Yes** 2000 MW
Areas for floating available in Maritime Spatial Plan	**Yes** Specific locations to be determined after stakeholder consultation	Yes	Yes	Yes	**Yes, but work is ongoing** The Offshore Renewable Energy Development Plan II identified areas for upcoming auction	No, but work is ongoing	Yes	No, but work is ongoing
Consult stakeholders	Yes	Yes	Yes	Yes	Yes	Under consideration	Yes	Under consideration
One-stop shop authority	Partially	Yes	Under consideration	Under consideration	Under consideration	No	No	No
Technology specific auctions	Yes	Partially	Yes	Under consideration	Under consideration	Under consideration	Under consideration	Under consideration
Rounds frequency, volumes, and evaluation criteria	Yes	Yes	Yes	Under consideration	Under consideration	Under consideration	Under consideration	Under consideration
Support for supply chain, ports, and mass production	**Partially** Recovery plan budget for greener ports	Yes	Under consideration	**Partially** Recovery plan budget for R&I	Under consideration	No	Under consideration	No
Grid connection roles and responsibilities	Yes	Yes	Yes	Yes	Yes	Under consideration	Under consideration	Under consideration

Source: WindEurope, 2023

A reliable, diversified, and sustainable offshore wind supply chain

Until the country builds its own supply chain for parts that can be sourced locally, there will be some element of foreign capital and technology in the early offshore wind projects in the Philippines. To build a reliable, well-diversified and sustainable offshore wind supply chain, the Philippines can integrate supply chain planning early on in its key industrial trade policies. This will also allow for the development of needed onshore supporting infrastructure (see Long-term vision and strategy).

A reliable supply chain

A reliable supply chain needs a predictable timeline of auctions that gives a medium-term visibility to investors. Offshore wind projects have a development time frame of up to seven years, of which two to three years is in construction. Based on this project timeline, a lead time between auctions and commercial operations of three to six years can be assumed. With governments around the world raising their clean energy ambitions, there might be competition in critical technology components, as well as securing vessel contracts. The fully booked foundation manufacturers in Europe for the next three years is an example of shortages that wind energy supply chains may face (WindEurope, 2023[32]). Setting up long-term agreements and partnerships with suppliers can hedge some of these insecurities, but this needs a strong investment pipeline and long-term visibility on auctions.

A well-diversified supply chain

In addition to reliability, the supply chain will need to be well diversified for the country to achieve an uninterrupted supply of components and materials, and avoid any construction delays. Disruptions in the solar PV sector caused by the zero-Covid policy in China reflect the importance of reducing dependency on one single country. Therefore, it is important for the Philippines to also develop local capabilities to have a wide selection of suppliers. In line with this, an overarching industrial policy that goes beyond the actual offshore wind projects, could bring economic benefits and a diversified supply chain.

A sustainable supply chain

Sustainability issues in the supply chain can be a key battleground for policy makers and international companies with high non-financial disclosure standards. The Philippines has regulations in place for promoting responsible business conduct (OECD, 2016[33]). Mainstreaming economic, social, and environmental metrics, combined with a clear communication strategy on business expectations can help the country manage issues in the supply chain and assess the impact on local communities. (OECD, 2016[33]). Closely linked to the sustainability of the supply chain is the consideration of environmental and social criteria in the project planning phase.

Availability and cost of capital

The scale of financing needed between now and 2040 for the Philippines to meet its offshore wind potential is estimated to reach USD 50 billion (World Bank, 2022[1]). Alongside policy, regulations and enabling infrastructure, questions on availability and cost of capital are also at the forefront of offshore wind discussions in the Philippines. Experience from other established offshore wind markets has shown that cost reductions were also possible thanks to the financial optimisation that happened at the transaction level (Guillet, 2022[9]).

The overall policy and macro-economic context will impact the cost of finance[2]

The availability and cost of capital in the Philippines will largely depend on the regulatory framework, administrative set-up in planning and permitting, grid development and a strong understanding of project and country risks by financiers.

The general macroeconomic conditions where the first projects will happen is also very important. The favourable financial context with "lower for longer" interest rates has come to an end. Increasing central bank rates to curb inflation have replaced the low-cost-money era. The Philippines has had one of Asia's most aggressive interest rate hikes, but currently the outlook stands stable at 6.25% (Reuters, 2023[34]).

Types of funding and financial structures will also impact the cost of finance[1]

The way a project is funded will also have an impact on the cost of capital and the contractual obligations, with the choice of instruments determined by the type of developer. Utilities and the domestic integrated conglomerates in the Philippines would typically opt for a corporate finance deal, largely based on equity with debt raised at corporate level. These companies can have access to low-cost finance thanks to strong balance sheet positions, diversified asset base and, most importantly, experience building and operating utility scale power plants.

Project finance transactions, funded by a consortium of debt and equity providers, can play a bigger role for smaller developers, independent power producers and international investors who lack local experience. As such, partnerships from a very early stage are key in project finance transactions. Due to the non-recourse nature of these deals and the strict requirements that come with co-ordinating a club of lenders, the cost of capital in these transactions can be higher when compared to corporate finance.

Project finance in the Philippines has been successfully deployed in large scale infrastructure projects, mostly public private partnerships. In the wind energy sector, project finance transactions have been deployed mostly for the refinancing of construction costs. Despite the willingness of lenders to take on construction risk, delays with the disbursement of the tariff meant that project sponsors had to take projects through early construction on equity.

Some non-recourse financing has been structured as dual currency transactions offered by a mix of local and international banks. Such transactions can facilitate knowledge transfer and capacity building indomestic institutions, improved risk perceptions and consequently a lower cost of finance over time (ADB, 2019[35]). Several offshore wind WESC holders in the Philippines have launched calls to form equity partnerships for project development, indicating a strong activity for project finance transactions.

Key actors financing offshore wind in the Philippines

Experience with other renewable energy technologies has shown a liquid debt market, with over 20 banks active, mostly domestic. Availability of capital has not been an issue, but the mixed ownership structures and conglomerate linkages may present some limitations on the domestic lending in the context of the GW scale – billion USD deals.

Moreover, financiers may remain cautious in the absence of an industry track record. There will be some implementation uncertainties and perceived risks that will be reflected in the financing structures as premium on credit spreads and insurance quotes.

Therefore, it is important to bring a diversity of financial actors with different risk profiles, for every stage of project development. Expanding the investor base would diversify the supply and sources of capital (McKinsey & Company, 2017[36]).

Long-term institutional investors have an investment profile that matches that of offshore wind. They look for long-term exposure to stable, cash generating assets, which fit the characteristics of renewable energy assets. Their role is particularly important in post-construction phase as they free up developer capital for new projects. If these refinancings are incorporated early in the financial assumptions, they can have a positive impact on the cost of capital and ultimately the bid prices (Guillet, 2022[9]).

More **active investors** such as hedge funds can help with both liquidity and price stabilisation. Whereas other private-market investors can provide capital to fund early-stage businesses and new technologies.

Insurance companies with offshore wind market knowledge are needed to provide an all-round coverage. Lenders would assume a worst-case scenario and typically look for insurance that covers all transactions linked to transport, storage, construction, operations and potential business interruption scenarios. This can be provided by a club of insurance companies that come together in the same transaction.

Multilateral and development bank (MDB) finance will continue to be important in financing higher risk operations and providing larger ticket sizes compared to commercial lenders. The World Bank estimates that concessional finance alone – for up to 16% of the project's capital expenditure – can lower the cost of electricity produced from offshore wind by 13%, down to USD 94/MWh from 108 USD/MWh. Blended with an additional 10% in grants of the project's capital expenditure, the cost of electricity decreases further by 35%, to reach USD 70/MWh (World Bank, 2023[37]). However, participation of MDBs may come with restrictions and reporting requirements that can delay the financing (ADB, 2019[35]). This can be an issue especially for project finance transactions, where all banks are required to move at the same pace and on equal terms. Lessons learned from previous onshore wind project finance transactions with multilateral development banks show some scope to apply a case-by-case analysis for key projects of national interests. Moreover, concessional finance from MDBs for strategic infrastructure will need to be available in terms that are more favourable than those of commercial banks.

Export Credit Agencies (ECAs) are another avenue to crowd in capital. Given that offshore wind manufacturing companies are already concentrated in Northern Europe, offshore wind projects in the Philippines would easily be able to demonstrate export value, thus creating an ideal opportunity to work with ECAs from that region. ECAs can provide highly rated credit guarantees covering up to 100% of the financing risks and with long risk coverage periods (up to 18 years). From industry consultations in the country, credit guarantees were considered as the most effective de-risking instrument for initial offshore wind projects during a poll.

Given the expected role that project finance can have in the offshore wind market in the Philippines, a closer consideration is needed at the comfort level with construction risk for each of the key financial actors in the industry. Non-recourse debt will typically include construction risk. MDBs and ECAs can play a significant role in providing financial support for offshore wind. However, they may have varying degrees of experience and expertise in managing construction risks for offshore wind farms. This can be accentuated by the level of complexity and the novelty of offshore wind in the Philippines. As such, training and capacity development on offshore wind market, technology and project phases from design to operation could be of added value in addressing some of the perceived risks.

Box 2.5. An overview of typical structures, investors, pricing and expected returns from existing offshore wind farms in Europe

The examples below from established offshore wind markets in the North Sea reflect decreasing risk perceptions from early phases to a maturing industry. It should be noted that country risk and the lack of track record in the Philippines may be reflected as a premium on margins and returns. It should also be noted that the projects below have been financed in a favourable macroeconomic context of low interest rates. With central banks increasing base rates to curb inflation, loan pricing has also changed.

Figure 2.5. Investor risk profiles and expected equity returns

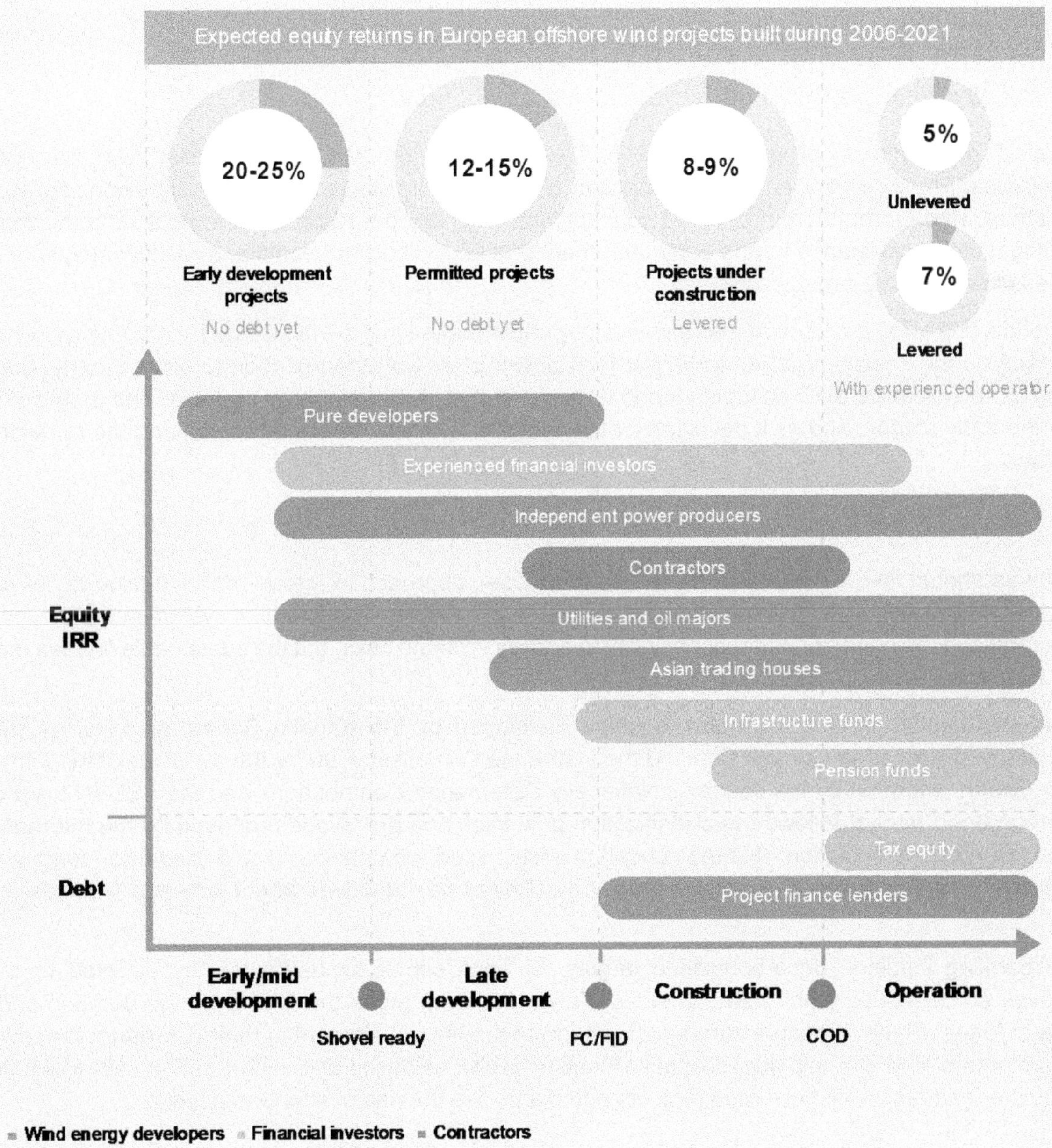

Source: (Guillet, 2022[9])

Table 2.5. Loan pricing in established offshore wind markets in Europe

Typical project finance in European offshore wind	Leverage	Maturity post-completion	Pricing	Maximum underwriting
2006-2007	60:40	10-15 years	150-200 bps	EUR 50-100 mln
2009-2013	65:35	10-15 years	300-350 bps	EUR 30-75 mln
2014-2015	70:30	10-15 years	200-250 bps	EUR 100-200 mln
2016-2017	75:25	15-17 years	150-225 bps	EUR100-150 mln
2018-2019	75:25	15-18 years	120-175 bps	EUR 100-150 mln

Source: (Guillet, 2022[9])

Dedicated financial instruments from development banks

Dedicated programmes of development banks can also redirect some capital towards cleaner technologies. The Energy Transition Mechanism (ETM) was highlighted as a potential financing avenue for offshore wind in the future. The ETM concept was originally developed by the ADB as a mechanism providing multilateral finance for the early retirement of coal-fired power plants and re-investments of cash proceeds in renewable energy projects.

The world's first ETM transaction was successfully implemented in the Philippines by AC Energy, wherein they divested the shares of a 246 MW coal-fired power plant with the intention to retire it early, thereby halving its technical life and recouping funds to reinvest in renewable energy projects. The programme is still in the early stages, and as it develops it also needs to address the social capital and the retraining of workforce.

Enabling sustainable finance regulations

Regulators should take a multi-sectoral and market-based approach to "green" policymaking to deliver an all-inclusive transition with sustainability and circularity at its heart. The financial system in the Philippines has recognised the need and the responsibility to address climate risks, but the sustainable finance market is still nascent.

A local sustainable finance taxonomy is being developed by the Bangko Sentral ng Pilipinas (BSP), Securities and Exchange Commission and the Insurance Commission under the auspices of the Financial Sector Forum, informed by the country's Nationally Determined Contributions and the ASEAN taxonomy. The green bond market follows the classification principles and guidelines proposed by the International Capital Markets Association (ICMA). Local publicly listed companies would need to comply with sustainability reporting guidelines released by the Philippine Securities and Exchange Commission in 2019.

In the banking industry, decarbonisation targets for each sector exposure can be adopted to create incentives on both supply and demand sides. These can help guide the financing, the duration and the pricing of loans. Equity investors can equally integrate the impact element in their risk-return frameworks for investments. This will help guide capital allocation decisions based on a long-term horizon which better reflects the features of offshore wind projects and minimises the risk of stranded assets.

Box 2.6. Consortium financing for offshore wind projects in Chinese Taipei

Loan syndication and consortium finance have been central in offshore wind financing in Chinese Taipei since the demonstration phase began in 2012. However, the composition of these financing vehicles is changing, from being mainly led by international financial institutions to seeing a growing involvement of local equity and debt financiers.

For instance, Formosa 1, a 128 MW demonstration phase offshore wind farm, was financed by a 16-year banking facility set up by three international lead project sponsors – Macquarie Capital (50%), Orsted (35%), and Swancor (15%). Eleven banks, both international and domestic, participated in this facility and had raised USD 613 million at the time of financial close in 2018.

Similarly, the 589 MW Changfang and Xidao offshore wind project was financed by a consortium of 25 international and domestic banks and financial institutions, with six export credit agencies providing credit guarantees. This project, owned by Copenhagen Infrastructure Partners with minor stakes held by two local life insurance companies, had raised a total of USD 3 billion by financial close in 2020.

On the other hand, the 298 MW Zhong Neng project is owned by China Steel Corporation (51%) and Copenhagen Infrastructure Partners (49%), thus becoming the first offshore wind project in the country with a local lead sponsor. USD 1.6 billion was raised in equity and debt financing by the lead sponsors and a consortium of 20 local and international banks.

Source: (Yates and Leybourne, 2019[38])

Roadmap to 2030

Policy recommendations

Enabling tools

Key recommendations for the Government of the Philippines to strengthen domestic enabling conditions for investment in offshore wind power include:

Taking a multi-sectoral and market-based approach to "green" policymaking, integrating political, economic, societal, and environmental factors for an all-inclusive transition with sustainability and circularity at its heart.

i. A whole-of-government approach can ensure that socio-economic development plans, maritime spatial plans, renewable energy development plans, power development plans, transmission and distribution development plans at central government and local level are coherent and aligned with each other, capitalizing on the high fixed and floating offshore wind potential.

ii. This can be complemented with efforts from government and international development partners to attract and re-train the local workforce for new careers in offshore wind, and more broadly the renewables sector, across all the supply chain.

Ensuring the DOE formulates a long-term vision and strategy for offshore wind under the 2023-2050 Philippine Energy Plan (PEP) that balances the country's energy transition with economic feasibility.

i. Clear, specific and time-bound targets under PEP 2023-2050 can enable both the government and the industry to make informed investment decisions on the country's future electricity mix and the strategic infrastructure, such as transmission grids and offshore wind ports.

ii. Different targets for fixed and floating offshore wind can reflect the different technological maturity stages, cost structures, revenue potentials and the specific infrastructure needs for each of these technologies.

Data driven zone allocation for fixed and floating offshore wind can fast track new projects, guide grid planning and improve procedures for transmission expansion and port upgrades.

i. In the short term, a collaborative effort led by the DOE, in partnership with the National Mapping and Resource Information Authority (NAMRIA), can consolidate and publish existing bathymetric and geological data collected under previous offshore oil and gas field projects.

ii. Subsequently, this database can be complemented with other relevant topographical data such as earthquake or typhoon risks, along with spatial maps of areas unavailable for commercial use, like shipping routes or military zones, not yet available on NAMRIA digital platforms.

iii. As a next step, future Marine Spatial Planning initiatives led by relevant government bodies can incorporate comprehensive mapping of marine ecosystems and endangered species, surveys of local fishing communities in high-resource areas, assessments of port and shipyard infrastructure, and evaluations of optimal access to global or regional supply chains.

Increased efforts on upgrades for key supporting infrastructure such as ports, which are crucial to the success of offshore wind development and the growth of the local supply chain.

i. Effective coordination among regional port authorities, local and central government, and other offshore wind planning agencies, is crucial for upgrading priority ports. A multiport strategy, where different ports collaborate to provide different services during a project's lifecycle, can be considered to facilitate finance and investments.

ii. Given the strategic nature of ports, these investments can be funded with a combination of public and private capital, supported by concessional finance. Concessional finance is crucial to financing the long-term investments in ports, which mostly rely on working capital and short-term finance for their normal operations.

iii. As with other long-term investments, securing financing for ports relies on a viable business case that can only be achieved with a frontloaded auction schedule, a timely planning and permitting, and specific offshore wind development zone allocation.

Strategic alignment between the DOE, the NGCP and the ERC is needed to address challenges in the planning, development and ownership of grid connection.

i. Accelerating the grid expansion and enhancing its efficiency are crucial in the Philippines for seamlessly integrating offshore wind into the power generation mix. This can help prevent congestions and curtailed power, as such improving the economic viability of offshore wind projects. The successful implementation of the centralised national grid project, connecting the country's three main regions, is pivotal to achieving these goals.

ii. A clearer role for the DOE in project selection and endorsement for the Transmission Development Plan, can expedite approvals and help avoid connection delays.
iii. Proactive grid planning - jointly by the DOE and the NGCP - for larger volumes of offshore wind capacity additions, can lower the cost per project along with the investments needed for onshore grid upgrades.
iv. Financing grid innovation alongside expansion and upgrade, led by the NGCP and TransCo in collaboration with the industry, is essential for cost-efficient renewables integration.
v. Given the high transmission costs of building and operating the connection to shore – a cost the developer may need to assume - a transparent methodology for allocating the fair market price under the recovery mechanism needs to be made available by the ERC.
vi. Supplementing current grid planning with a comprehensive study to assess grid readiness for integrating more renewable capacity can ensure the Philippine transmission grid meets the needs of the growing renewable energy market.

Carefully reflecting the unique characteristics of offshore wind projects will be central to ensuring the effectiveness of the offshore wind one-stop shop approach.

i. Early coordination and consultation with relevant stakeholders will ensure a timely implementation of the President's Executive Order on a dedicated offshore wind one-stop shop.
ii. A comprehensive review involving all necessary agencies involved in permitting and planning can enhance transparency, efficiency, consistency in permitting requirements and reduce barriers to entry.
iii. Investing in adequate digital and human resources is essential to streamline the processes while keeping an open dialogue with the industry.
iv. The rule of positive silence currently in place for WESC award procedures is a constructive approach that could also benefit the offshore wind one-stop shop.

Setting the right regulatory framework is important to create and maintain a competitive industrial base, support a growing industry, and limit the impact on public finances.

i. Allocating offshore wind in a separate technology band in the Green Energy Auction Program can improve competition outcome. This can be complemented by an open-door policy for developer led deployments.
ii. Adequate visibility on timing, volumes and pricing will create a predictable project pipeline while supporting workforce and resource planning for vessel orders, component procurement and installation.
iii. Realistic auction deliverable timelines and carefully estimated pricing can ensure projects are built on time and at the lowest possible cost for both developers and society. As such, a transparent costing methodology needs to be developed by the ERC prior to establishing the GEAR auction prices.
iv. The auction tariffs (GEAR) will need to reflect a fair risk-sharing mechanism between the public sector and private developers, considering the country specific set-up for planning and permitting, provisions on transmission lines and support facilities in ports.
v. Corporate PPAs can be an additional revenue stream alongside policy support. Providing industry guidelines and tools for clear contractual terms minimises dispute resolution and counterparty risk under corporate PPAs.

Well-designed policies and regulations that go beyond the energy markets will be key to getting the financing right for offshore wind in the Philippines. Offshore wind investments fit well with the trends towards sustainable finance, which the Philippines is promoting in its regional fora.

i. The Philippines' offshore wind policy toolkit will need to strike a balance between predictability and adaptability to technological developments and macroeconomic shifts. Grandfathering clauses against retroactive policy changes is a good practice that can safeguard investment value and ensure low-cost capital is available.

ii. Multilateral and development banks can expedite key projects vital to national interests by streamlining internal procedures. Early project financings are crucial for setting market pace and risk perceptions, with multilateral finance playing a significant role in attracting commercial funding.

iii. First loss guarantees, which have been critical in boosting Europe's offshore wind competitiveness, may be replicated in the Philippines through similar blended finance instruments offered by multilateral financial institutions.

iv. It is important to bring a diversity of financiers with different risk profiles, for every stage of project development. This can help the industry recycle capital and free up more resources for new projects. Billion USD scale financing will require more domestic and international lenders and investors.

v. International partners can collaborate with the Banking Association of the Philippines (BAP) and institutional investors to offer targeted training and capacity building programmes for domestic financial institutions. This can help the sector improve the understanding of offshore wind energy markets, risks and properly price any related financing.

vi. Financial markets, in particular banks, can have dedicated targets for the decarbonisation of their portfolios. BSP expects banks to set their strategic environmental and social objectives. This can help guide the financing, the duration, and the pricing of loans for renewable energy projects.

References

ADB (2019), *EDC Burgos Wind Power Corporation*. [35]

BusinessWorld (2023), *First PHL offshore wind project cleared for green lane treatment*, https://www.bworldonline.com/economy/2023/12/21/565207/first-phl-offshore-wind-project-cleared-for-green-lane-treatment/#:~:text=THE%20Board%20of%20Investments%20(BoI,processing%20of%20permits%20and%20licenses. [7]

BVG Associates (n.d.), *Wind farm costs*, https://guidetoanoffshorewindfarm.com/wind-farm-costs (accessed on 7 February 2023). [11]

Dixson-Declève, S. (2022), *It takes longer to permit a wind farm than to build it*, https://www.euractiv.com/section/energy-environment/opinion/it-takes-longer-to-permit-a-wind-farm-than-to-build-it/. [14]

DOE (2023), *Executive Order No.21*, https://www.doe.gov.ph/laws-and-issuances/executive-order. [5]

DOE (2023), *Notice of Auction - Green Energy Auction-2 (GEA-2) for Renewable Energy (RE)*. [13]

DOE (2022), *Advisory on the Enhancement of Policies and Guidelines for the Development of Offshore Wind Projects*, https://www.doe.gov.ph/announcements/advisory-enhancement-policies-and-guidelines-development-offshore-wind-projects. [3]

DOE (2021), *Green Energy Auction Program in the Philippines*. [21]

ERC (2022), *ERC Raises Alarm Over Complaints from Contestable Customers*. [23]

EVOSS (2023), *Energy Virtual One Stop Shop*. [6]

Fitch Solutions (2022), *Floating Wind On The Cusp Of Global Commercial Growth With A Thriving Competitive Landscape*, https://www.fitchsolutions.com/renewables/floating-wind-cusp-global-commercial-growth-thriving-competitive-landscape-01-06-2022?fSWebArticleValidation=true&mkt_tok=NzMyLUNLSC03NjcAAAGODdQQ52xWCCBysS_lLMb7kRYNhoznaXF5pXjC2XNf0aJECdHHHWw4oiR5LktufHlJ5pJXfmY (accessed on 9 July 2023). [20]

Florence School of Regulation (2023), *Contracts-for-Difference*. [31]

Guillet, J. (2022), *Financing Offshore Wind*. [9]

IEA (2022), *Cost of Capital Observatory*. [10]

IEA (2022), *Smart Grids*. [28]

IRENA (2022), *Renewable Energy Auctions Southeast Asia*. [17]

IRENA (2022), *Renewable Power Generation Costs in 2021*. [4]

Janipour, Z. (2023), *The Bottlenecks Challenging Growth in the EU Offshore Wind Supply Chain*. [18]

Jansen, M. et al. (2022), "Policy choices and outcomes for offshore wind auctions globally", *Energy Policy*, https://doi.org/10.1016/j.enpol.2022.113000. [29]

JRC (2022), *RePowerEU: new mapping tool supports identification of go–to areas for renewables*, https://joint-research-centre.ec.europa.eu/jrc-news-and-updates/repowereu-new-mapping-tool-supports-identification-go-areas-renewables-2022-05-18_en (accessed on 2023). [27]

Lee, A. (2023), *Orsted wins green light for 'utility scale' battery plant linked to giant North Sea wind farm*, ReCharge, https://www.rechargenews.com/energy-transition/orsted-wins-green-light-for-utility-scale-battery-plant-linked-to-giant-north-sea-wind-farm/2-1-1386744. [30]

McKinsey & Company (2017), "Deepening capital markets in the Philippines", *Featured Insights*, https://www.mckinsey.com/featured-insights/asia-pacific/deepening-capital-markets-in-the-philippines (accessed on 2 March 2023). [36]

Mercurio, R. (2022), *DOE crafts EO for offshore wind development*, https://www.philstar.com/business/2022/11/13/2223383/doe-crafts-eo-offshore-wind-development. [26]

NARDAC (2023), "Cost of insuring offshore wind", *NARDAC Quarterly Newsletter*, https://vimeo.com/867710206/8361fd8078 (accessed on October 2023). [19]

NGCP (2022), *Transmission Development Plan 2022-2040*. [16]

OECD (2022), *OECD Clean Energy Finance and Investment Consultation Workshop*, https://www.oecd.org/environment/cc/cefim/philippines/secondoecd-doeworkshopunlockingfinanceandinvestmentforcleanenergyinthephilippines.htm (accessed on 2023). [15]

OECD (2022), *Second OECD-DOE Workshop: Unlocking finance and investment for clean energy in the Philippines*. [8]

OECD (2016), *Finance and Investment Policy Review for the Philippines*. [33]

Reuters (2023), *Expanding Ports to Achieve Large-Scale Offshore Wind Deployment*. [25]

Reuters (2023), "Philippine central bank signals pause in rate hikes in May", https://www.reuters.com/markets/asia/philippine-central-bank-signals-pause-rate-hikes-may-2023-04-12/. [34]

Shliomenzon, Y. (2022), *S&P Global*. [12]

WESM (2023), "Quarterly Retail Market Assessment Report", *Market Surveillance Committee*, https://www.wesm.ph/market-outcomes/retail-market-assessment-reports/quarterly-retail-market-assessment-report (accessed on September 2023). [22]

WindEurope (2023), *Offshore Wind Supply Chain Workshop*. [32]

WindEurope (2021), *A 2030 Vision for European Offshore Wind Ports*. [24]

World Bank (2023), *Concessional Climate Finance Essential to Catalyzing Offshore Wind Development in Emerging Markets*. [37]

World Bank (2022), *A Roadmap for Offshore Wind in the Philippines*. [1]

World Bank (2022), *Offshore Wind Roadmap for the Philippines*, https://documents1.worldbank.org/curated/en/099225004192234223/pdf/P1750040b777da0c30935a0e2aa346f4e26.pdf. [2]

Yates, C. and M. Leybourne (2019), "Financing Offshore Wind in Taiwan", *Journal of National Development Studies*, https://www.researchgate.net/publication/336278344_Financing_Offshore_Wind_in_Taiwan (accessed on January 2023). [38]

Notes

[1] Contestable customers are large end-users that can purchase power directly from suppliers or RES under the retail competition and open access program (RCOA) under Republic Act No. 9136 or EPIRA.

[2] Unless otherwise stated, this section is based on authors' analysis from Clean Energy Pipeline financial transactions in the Philippines since 2008. This includes new asset finance, refinancing transactions, mergers and acquisitions and capital market transactions. To the extent possible, transactions capture all clean energy technologies in the Philippines, including storage and self-generation. Energy efficiency transactions are not included.

3 Innovative funding and business models for energy efficiency in public buildings

The Philippines already has legislation in place to support energy efficiency initiatives by the public sector. The country is rapidly catching up on demand-side productivity and efforts are underway to kick-start an energy efficiency market in the Philippines. The results to date are mixed, with limited uptake by local government units and agencies as principal target adopters. This chapter focuses on energy efficiency actions that may facilitate or accelerate adoption, particularly for public buildings. It addresses the enabling conditions and the financing tools needed to accelerate the development of an energy efficiency market, which remains nascent despite the different measures that have been adopted under the Energy Efficiency and Conservation Act.

The building sector in the Philippines is one of the largest consumers of electricity in the country, with roughly 15-20% of nationwide electric power consumption. Under the 2017-40 Energy Efficiency and Conservation Plan, the Philippines aims to achieve annual reductions of 1.2% and 1.9% in energy consumption within the residential and commercial sectors, which includes public buildings.

The government is also expected to play a key role in taking the lead to institutionalise and promote energy efficiency and conservation across all sectors in the country. One of the measures that was particularly strengthened under the Energy Efficiency and Conservation Law of 2019 is the implementation of the Government Energy Management Program (GEMP). The GEMP requires all government offices, including Local Government Units (LGUs) to reduce monthly electricity and petroleum products consumption by 10%, compared to 2004 and 2005 levels.

In support of these initiatives, the DOE issued a set of guidelines in May 2023 for strengthening skills and capacities for Energy Efficiency and Conservation (EEC) professionals[1]. These guidelines include the appointment of EEC coordinators in all government agencies, tasked with assisting EEC Officers and focal staff in implementing energy efficiency and conservation measures in their own offices/buildings. Additionally, the guidelines encompass the adoption of training modules and a certification process to recognize training institutions, reinforcing skills and capacity building for EE&C professionals in the public sector.

The government maintains that a successful implementation of the GEMP will set an example for the Philippine energy efficiency market, which currently remains in its infancy. As of 31 May 2023, the public sector has recorded a total electricity savings of 20.67 million kWh throughout the duration of the GEMP. This shows the potential of government buildings in terms of energy efficiency and conservation.

Despite these developments, the GEMP faces challenges in achieving widespread compliance. To date, just under half of government entities are compliant. This roadmap chapter focuses on near- and medium-term actions to incentivise higher energy efficiency amongst LGUs.

Energy efficiency market developments and trends to date

The government maintains that a successful implementation of the GEMP will set an example for the Philippine energy efficiency market. To provide strategic direction, improve the adoption and accelerate the implementation of the GEMP, the EE&C act mandated the creation of the Inter-Agency Energy Efficiency and Conservation Committee (IAEECC). The IAEECC is chaired by the DOE and has eight government member agencies, namely: the National Economic and Development Authority (NEDA); the Departments of Budget and Management; Finance; Public Works and Highways; Science and Technology; the Interior and Local Government; Trade and Industry; and Transportation. Since 2020, the IAEECC has issued a total of seven resolutions which serve as a guide to all government entities to further the implementation of the EE&C in the public sector (see Annex A).

Under the IAEECC GEMP guidelines issued in 2022, government entities are provided with two financing options to pursue energy efficiency projects in their buildings. To carry out their own Government Energy Efficiency Projects (GEEPs) government entities can choose between the Energy Service Companies (ESCO's) -based and the Public Sector-Led financial models. The former allows government entities to commission ESCOs through Energy Savings Performance Contracts (ESPCs). The latter allows government entities to implement, fund and/or finance GEEPs without an ESCO and ESPC.

To date, several government entities have chosen to enter an ESPC with an ESCO and have already completed their energy efficiency projects. An example of this is the Commission on Audit Main Office

[1] On 12 May 2023, the DOE issued Department Circular (DC) 2023-05-0009, or the GEMP implementing guidelines.

which entered into an ESPC with the Philippine National Oil Company - Renewables Corporation (PNOC-RC) to realise their solar rooftop project.

Furthermore, the DOE is currently drafting updates to the Green Building Code, which should provide further guidance for the construction and retrofitting of buildings. The code will notably define energy efficiency and conservation guidelines for buildings with total floor area of areas more than 10 000 square feet and mandate them to have certified energy efficiency officers or managers. All new building permits (including public buildings) will be bound by these guidelines.

The measures taken so far have generated government savings of an estimated USD 3.7 million as of the first quarter of 2023. Energy efficient technology has been the main driver of these savings, not only for LED lighting but also for cooling via inverter-type air conditioners (Business World Online, 2022[1]). The government is setting the example, but the private sector has also awakened to the potential of energy savings. In addition to 7 441 identified government entities, there are also over 4 000 designated private sector establishments - including commercial, industrial and transportation sectors - implementing various projects to reduce their energy consumption to date.

On the institutional front, the DOE is setting up an energy management team, responsible for adopting a systems approach to boosting the implementation of energy efficiency and conservation measures. This will include a co-ordinated effort to implement energy efficiency, energy use and energy consumption activities. Government commitment has attracted the interest of international investors with proven technologies and experience in energy efficiency.

Growth potential and investment needs

Achieving the Philippines EE&C Roadmap 2023-2050's aspirational targets requires mobilising a substantial amount of both public and private capital. The Philippines Energy Efficiency Alliance (PE2), for instance, estimated that achieving the EE&C Roadmap targets by 2040 would require a total USD 243 billion or around USD 10.5 billion annually – an amount roughly 36 times greater than the cumulative energy efficiency investment realised over 2019-21 (around USD 97.7 million annually).

While there is no official estimate of investment needs for energy efficiency in the public sector, existing evidence seems to point to a considerable potential. For instance, according to analysis based on energy data of 178 public buildings,[1] upgrading their lighting and air conditioning could help generate PHP 705 million (USD 13 million) of annual savings (equivalent to a 33% reduction in annual electricity consumption or 85 million kWh). This investment would cost an estimated PHP 2.2 billion (USD 39 million) with an average payback period of 3.5 years (World Bank, 2018[2]). This only represents a subset of all existing public buildings. As such, actual energy savings in the public sector are likely to be higher. Creating the right enabling conditions is thus crucial to reap the benefits of that potential.

Box 3.1. Example from the Santa Rosa municipality

Santa Rosa is a 1st class component city located in the south of Luzon and inhabited by 414,812 people. The city has been a country pioneer in undertaking energy efficiency and conservation efforts and, as of late, making important progress towards the GEMP objectives.

Indeed, through the implementation of key energy efficiency measures, the city managed to reduce energy consumption. For instance, the installation of solar panels and the replacement of lighting fixtures to LED lights in one of its city hall building complexes in mid-2019, enabled a roughly 8% reduction in average power consumption (79,571 kwh in 2019) compared to a year prior (86,680 kwh in 2018). Other key measures were also implemented, such as the installation of LED metered streetlights, the conduct of regular awareness raising campaigns as well as the upgrade of energy consumption and equipment inventory data and information.

In addition, Santa Rosa is among the very few cities in the country to have adopted a Local Energy Code and formulated its Local Energy Efficiency and Conservation Plan (LEECP) with the Technical assistance of PLLENRO and USAID. It has also submitted a number of key documents related to its energy consumption (e.g. monthly electricity consumption report, and an inventory of office equipment, etc.) to the Department of Energy.

As discussed during the first OECD-DOE Roadmap workshop, the collection and monitoring of key data and metrics relative to the energy consumption of municipal buildings and vehicle fleets were particularly challenging. This was notably overcome through the allocation/recruitment of specific officers/staff to report on and monitor the energy consumption of, as well as inspect and maintain, municipality buildings, public street lighting and electric vehicle fleets. Educational campaigns are being further considered by Santa Rosa's LGU to continue improving both energy efficiency and data gathering.

Source: (OECD, 2022[3])

Energy efficiency development challenges in public buildings

Since the implementation of the EE&C Act, a few LGUs have made progress towards meeting the GEMP target, allocating resources to energy-efficiency-related research, planning, data collection, monitoring, and maintenance of equipment. These are already seeing results in the form of reduced energy bills. Equally, in some off-grid areas, with heavy reliance on expensive diesel, LGUs have made significant energy efficiency improvements to their equipment – not necessarily with the objective to comply with the GEMP but simply on the grounds that these are good financial investments.

As of the first half of 2023, the total awareness of government entities regarding EEC and the GEMP is at 41.86% based on the co-ordination meetings, information, education and communication campaigns and hands-on GEMP System trainings conducted by the DOE. Despite the awareness, LGUs still experience challenges in complying with the GEMP. Most notably, LGUs continue to face a significant shortage of skills and workforce capacity constraints. Further, LGUs often lack the capacity to plan and undertake energy efficiency projects, conduct energy audits, and do the necessary procurement (e.g. preparation of Request for Proposal/ technical specifications, technical review, bid evaluation, etc.).

To overcome this issue, awareness raising campaigns, capacity building and further incentives were highlighted during several stakeholder consultations as key efforts to support LGUs in adopting energy efficiency solutions and thereby achieve GEMP objectives. Still, other hurdles continue to set back compliance with the GEMP targets.

LGUs budgetary rules for energy efficiency

Budgetary constraint is one of the biggest challenges to the adoption of energy efficiency in the Philippines' public sector. While targets are ambitious, the Government has very limited budget to fund energy efficiency projects by itself, although it has set aside budget (at the central government level) to fund a few clean energy initiatives. For instance, it has implemented solar rooftop projects in three government buildings[2] and has allocated PHP 25 million in the 2023 budget to support energy audits for 160 LGUs.

Still, numerous LGUs do not have sufficient budget to invest in energy efficiency, particularly in poorer and remote areas. Hence, those having made most progress to date are often those LGUs with highest budget and/or those that benefitted from international development assistance. This is compounded by limited access to finance due to the poor financial health of certain LGUs, and the absence of a robust credit rating system for LGUs.

In theory, a solution to alleviate budget constraints, could be to use realised energy savings to repay capital expenditures – which can be funded by debt, leasing or budget. However, current budgetary rules generally disallow the ownership of energy savings, let alone re-using them to repay project's financial liabilities. Indeed, as budgets are prepared annually, and each annual budget allocation is based on the previous year's expenditures, any reduction in operating expenditures (i.e. from energy savings) would lead to a decrease in budget allocation the following year. This makes it difficult to repay loans (or leases) from realised energy savings or recover the budget used to fund the initial investment. Even worse, this creates a split incentive wherein the implementing LGUs do not retain the benefits of energy savings (i.e. increase budget availability) and hence, have little to no incentive to make energy efficiency improvements.

To address this issue, the DOE issued Department Circular (DC) 2022-04-0006, titled "Guidelines on the Endorsement of Government Energy Efficiency Projects to the IAEECC Pursuant to the GEMP Guidelines". This circular outlines the development of Government Energy Efficiency Projects (GEEPs), their implementation schemes, and the DOE's criteria for evaluating and approving GEEPs. The objective is to empower Local Government Units (LGUs) to allocate their own budgets for energy efficiency within the broader government budget.

Most notably, the circular enables LGUs to accrue and reuse freed-up budget from lower energy consumption (resulting from the implementation of energy conservation measures) for energy efficiency-related capital expenditures. In particular, LGUs that achieve more than 10% (or between 5% and 10%) reduction in energy consumption, are eligible to receive Energy Reduction Cost Certificates issued by the DOE. These certificates can be utilised to either repay or invest in new energy efficiency-related capital expenditures with up to 100% of savings.

While the use of budget with cost recovery should continue to be promoted, it is likely that LGUs implementing their first projects may have to use (at least part) of their own budget to cover investment costs. Given limited LGU budget, allocating greater share of government budget to LGUs while concomitantly diversifying sources of funding and raising additional funds for energy efficiency going forward -- such as through seed capital and by looking into innovative financing arrangements – is important. In this regard, the recent Mandanas ruling raises hope that LGUs may be given additional financial resources in the near future to invest in energy efficiency, although this is yet to materialise.

Harnessing Energy Performance Contracts (EPCs) in the public sector

EPCs are energy efficiency contract models under which a range of services (from project design to operation and maintenance/O&M) related to energy efficiency and conservation are provided to an end-user or its associated facilities by a private entity (typically, an ESCO). Under certain EPC models, the

ESCO can provide financing so that the host facility must disburse little to no capital upfront. In this kind of model, the capital is re-paid directly from energy savings, and hence is contingent on the performance of the installed equipment.

EPCs feature several key advantages that could help overcome some of the challenges mentioned above. Among other things, ESCOs can potentially (World Bank, 2010[4]):

- Help reduce transaction costs, bundling all of the various steps typically required to implement an energy efficiency project into one contract, thereby facilitating public procurement.
- Transfer technical/technology risks away from public end-users (and financiers) by providing project/equipment performance guarantees and offering O&M services to ensure that the installed equipment continues to perform at appropriate levels.
- Facilitate access to external capital and offer more flexible financing options for projects, thereby alleviating some of the budgetary constraints that public agencies typically face.

Different EPC models exist globally, of which the two most prevalent are the shared savings and guaranteed saving models, as part of which the ESCO performs most services from design to O&M. In the case of the shared savings EPC model, the ESCO also provides financing, which it reimburses from a percentage of realised energy savings. In the guaranteed savings model, the ESCO guarantees a minimum level of performance but, in turn, the end-user must obtain financing from a third-party, effectively taking on the financing risk. Preference between shared and guaranteed savings vary across countries and regions, often due to different national policy and accounting rules.

Still, a broader range of EPC models exist and have been used globally. The experience of China (one of the world's largest ESCO markets) shows that the variety of models used evolve as the energy efficiency market matures. Indeed, in 2012, guaranteed and shared savings represented more than 85% of the EPC market against 45% in 2019, the remainder being other forms of EPC models (Efficiency, 2020[5]).

Procurement of energy efficiency projects in the public sector

While EPC is an interesting option to facilitate the implementation of energy efficiency projects in public buildings, their public procurement has been particularly challenging. First, multiyear contracting, while legally possible, has proven particularly difficult in practice. This, in turn, affects the financial viability of energy efficiency projects whose payback period more than often exceeds a single year.

Other public procurement rules also make it difficult for LGUs to make energy efficiency improvements. A notable example is the Government Procurement Reform Act (Republic Act 9184) that only allows for the procurement of "pure goods" and "pure services" thereby disabling the procurement of mixed contracts such as energy performance contracts (EPCs) which typically provides bundled contracts. This means that the procurement of elements, typically covered under an EPC, such as (investment-grade) energy audits (to set up a baseline and evaluate potential improvements/investment potential) and equipment must be procured separately, effectively adding extra transaction cost and lead time.

Therefore, LGUs often prefer going through a government or public entity to do their energy audits as such procurement arrangements are far less cumbersome (e.g. no competitive tender is required). Public institutions such as the Philippines National Oil Company–Renewables Corporation (PNOC-RC), the DOE or the Department of Science and Technology (DOST) do provide energy consulting or auditing services to other government entities, among others. The DOE, for instance, has even set a target for itself to audit 100 government buildings in 2023 and for the PNOC-RC to audit around 380 of them.

While these are laudable efforts and actions, they remain small compared to actual number of entities requiring energy auditing. It is also clear that neither the PNOC-RC nor the government has the capacity to audit the 7,441 government entities covered under the GEMP, let alone fill the energy efficiency investment gap in public buildings. As of January 2023, for instance, the PNOC-RC had only audited 80 of the targeted 380 LGU buildings, although it had engaged and visited around 160 of them. Lack of LGUs' awareness and co-operation with regards to providing access to their facilities' data and information was also a key impediment to that. Equally, beyond auditing (which is key to identifying opportunities and creating an energy consumption baseline for evaluating energy savings), the PNOC-RC and the government have resources to invest, build and operate energy efficiency projects within government facilities.

Private ESCOs in the Philippines' public sector: state of play and key challenges

As mentioned before, private ESCOs could play a key role in supporting energy efficiency improvements in the Philippines' public sector, most notably through EPCs. Hence, significant efforts have been made to structure and accelerate the development of an ESCO market in the country. In 2020, the Department of Energy (DOE) issued a Department Circular 2020-09-0018 providing "Guidelines in the Administration Classification and Certification of ESCOs" in a bid to improve clarity and set standards for ESCOs. As per the circular, to be classified as an ESCO, a firm must be registered by the DOE, which is conditioned to meeting a set of basic criteria. Registered firms can also obtain certification, which guarantees a certain level of business (historical) performance. As of June 2022, (DoE, 2022[6]), there were 36 ESCOs in the country, a five-fold increase compared to 2015, of which only seven were certified. While this is an encouraging trend, in reality, only a few ESCOs actually undertake EPCs, which means they still need to develop their technical, business development, and risk management skills and capabilities. Over 2019-21, ESCOs represented 15% of total energy efficiency investment (roughly current USD 317 million), most of which occurred in commercial buildings.

Despite these efforts, the ESCO market in the Philippines remains in its infancy as it is beset by a number of challenges. Most notably, limited access to affordable finance remains one of the most pressing challenges for ESCOs in the country (DoF / LCEP, 2021[7]). Indeed, energy efficiency projects are often perceived as too small and/or risky by financial institutions, often leading them to require high levels of collateral.

While some banks have adopted dedicated financing programmes for which energy efficiency projects are eligible, energy efficiency practitioners consulted as part of the roadmap process continued to highlight difficulties in accessing finance. These include lack of capacity in developing bankable projects and eligibility criteria related to public debt ceilings that don't allow LGUs to access debt finance.

Equally, the ability to reliably verify energy savings and attribute such savings to the energy efficiency project is also a critical aspect to increase LGU/customer and investor confidence. Hence, ensuring the development of reliable verification systems and protocols (including from a third party) is important to ensure the bankability of investment-grade audits/EPC and avoid claims and counterclaims (at times leading to litigation).

Overall, the relatively low demand for energy efficiency, compared to the country's energy potential, is an important challenge, which hampers further expansion of the country's ESCO market. Hence, encouraging government demand for energy efficiency (e.g. through increased compliance with the GEMP) can help kickstart an ESCO market in the country, as has been the case in other jurisdictions. This may include the build-up of a project pipeline that creates a minimum market size and allows private sector ESCOs to gain the experience and track record of successful project implementation. A key pre-requisite for that, however, will be solving existing procurement constraints, among others.

Incentivising energy efficiency in public buildings

The absence of standards, challenges in securing an adequate workforce capacity, shortages of skills, and the LGU budgetary limitations are some of the main barriers to funding energy efficiency projects in the public building sector. Mechanisms that can support energy efficiency projects in public buildings can include:

- revisions of public procurement and accounting rules to enable investment in energy efficiency projects with payback periods exceeding one calendar year and allowing for bundled contracts
- mandatory, well-enforced building energy codes which cover all building types including new construction and existing buildings
- a focus on training, capacity building and social awareness campaigns across the value chain, including the financial sector
- concessional finance granted under favourable terms or intermediate lending from international financial institutions to local banks
- innovation pilot projects that can accelerate deployment based on market driven approaches.

It should be noted that the twin challenges of workforce capacity and adequate skills can be addressed a priori, to ensure a successful implementation of the pilot projects and their potential scale up. This is largely consistent with the need to broaden the scope of private sector participation in public building energy efficiency projects to include private contractors in anticipation of an accelerated deployment post pilot stage.

Public Super ESCO: a possible solution

International experience provides interesting insights into how other countries have worked around some of these well-known public procurement restrictions, and which could be adapted if not replicated in the Philippines' context. One example is the public ESCO model – also known as Super ESCO.

The Super ESCO model has been adopted by numerous countries, typically to kickstart the nascent, local energy efficiency market. Indeed, by supporting the adoption of energy efficiency solutions in the public sector (e.g. hospitals, schools, municipal utilities, government buildings and other public facilities), these have often supported the capacity development and project development activities of existing private ESCOs (e.g. subcontracting, reducing transaction costs, provision of financing, etc.). A key advantage of a public Super ESCO resides in the fact that these very often do not have to go through a (often cumbersome) public procurement/tendering process for project development, since in this case one public agency is simply contracting with another public entity. On the financing side, the super ESCO benefits from a greater creditworthiness compared to smaller private-sector ESCOs, leading to easier access to finance. Other advantages of the Super ESCO structure relate to project aggregation and standardisation, thereby lowering transaction costs and creating scale, while better meeting financier's requirements.

Figure 3.1. Illustration of typical activities of a Super ESCO

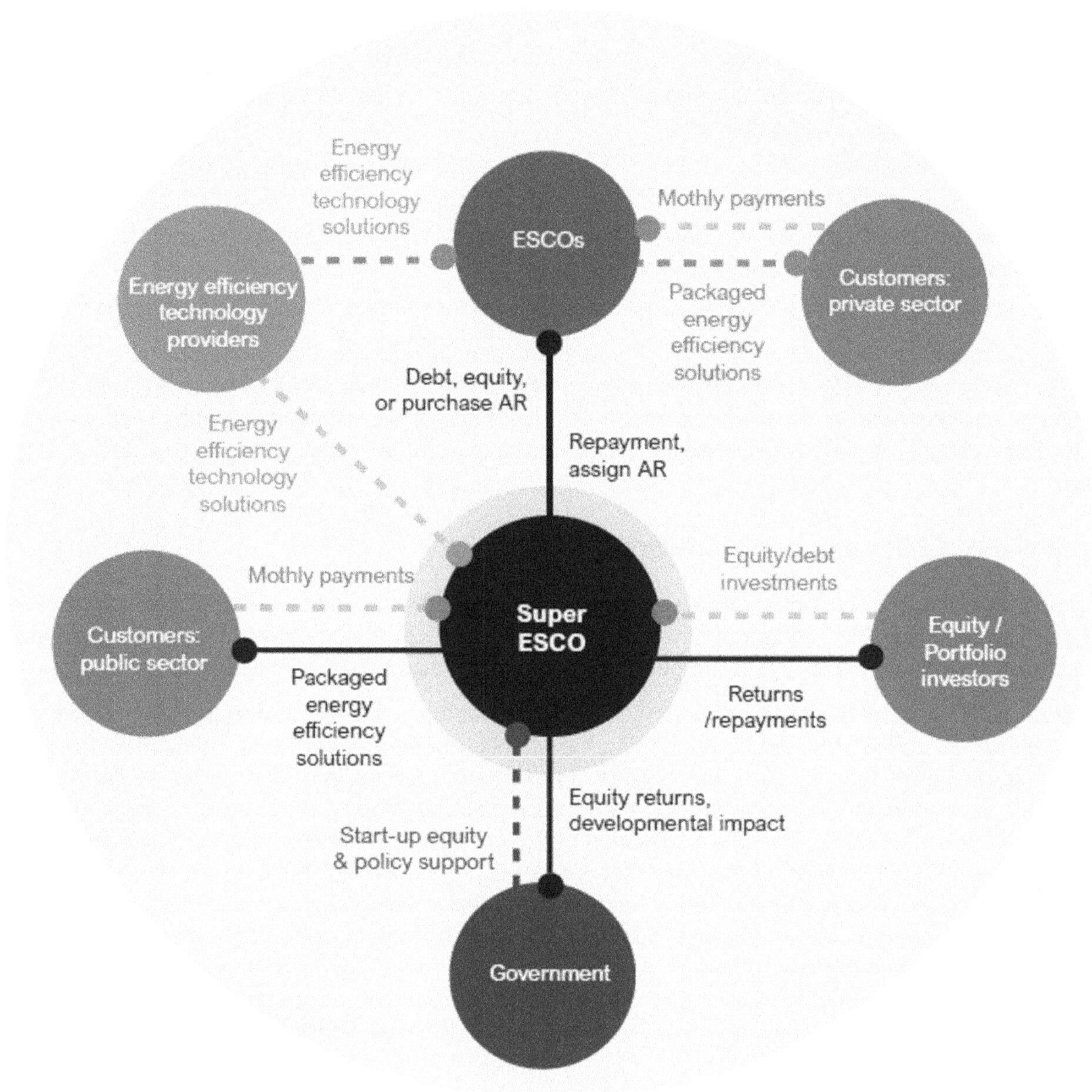

Note: ESCOs = energy service companies; ESPC = energy savings performance contract; FIs = financial institutions; M&V = measurement and verification.
Source: (World Bank, 2018[8]).

There are variations in the way Super ESCOs operate globally, both in terms of structure and operations. In China, for instance, state-owned ESCOs (also known as energy management companies) were established to act as for-profit ESCOs whose initial role was to support the development of the country's energy efficiency market, focusing largely on the industry sector.

In Croatia, a super ESCO was established within the country's public power utility to support local government institutions' uptake of energy efficiency projects. In other countries, the Super ESCO has had a more traditional role, acting as the main (if not the sole) responsible entity for energy efficiency project implementation in public facilities, subcontracting work to private ESCOs (e.g. in Saudi Arabia or United

Arab Emirates). In India, for instance, the Energy Efficiency Services Limited – or EESL, the country's Super ESCO – has played a key role in facilitating energy efficiency project development in the public and residential sectors, including through large-scale procurement programmes to reduce transaction costs through aggregation, and through providing financing solutions for end users. Global examples of Super ESCOs are highlighted in Box 3.2.

The Super ESCO concept is not new to the Philippines. In 2008, the state owned PNOC-RC was established as a subsidiary of the PNOC (the national oil and gas company) to provide clean energy services, including energy efficiency. Taking on the role of a public Super ESCO, and using a shared-saving model, the plan was for PNOC-RC to provide financing and technical services, and conduct the operation and maintenance of equipment for public agencies, in exchange for an agreed-upon monthly fee. To implement its energy efficiency and demand-side management projects, PNOC-RC would be allowed to subcontract private ESCOs (through competitive tender) with the objective to help develop an ESCO market. It also was to undertake information and education campaigns and conduct forums on energy efficiency and conservation. However, the role of PNOC-RC remained only within energy efficiency consulting and energy audit services. Acting as a Super ESCO would have important budget implications to be considered due to the significant resources and increased institutional capacity required.

More recently, private sector initiatives have taken the role of the aggregator entity in the Philippines. Climargy is a private sector initiative in the Philippines that serves as a commercial Super ESCO aggregator of ESCO project assets, fully funded with private capital. Climargy is also tapping into grant funding through a partnership with UNOPS Southeast Asia Energy Transition Partnership. The company is planning to use these grants to subsidise and de-risk the upfront development costs of energy audits for energy efficiency projects in commercial and industrial entities (UNEPCCC, 2023[9]).

Box 3.2. Some global examples of public Super ESCO models

- China's Energy Management Companies (EMCs) were initially created by the government, with support from the World Bank and the Global Environment Facility, in three municipalities. These EMCs first targeted the most energy-intensive industries, such as cement and iron and steel, to maximise their energy-saving benefits. They also implemented EPC contracts in the public sector. In the face of their early success, other state-owned ESCOs emerged, helping grow the energy efficiency market in China. The creation of the EMC Association in 2003 further helped accelerate the ESCO market development including through industry self-regulation (e.g. document standardisation, etc.), capacity building, knowledge sharing and fostering business collaboration.
- The HEP ESCO in Croatia was established in 2003, with support from the World Bank and the Global Environment Facility, within the country's national power utility, Hrvatska Elektroprivreda d.d. (HEP) with the objective of developing, financing and implementing energy efficiency projects on a commercial basis, tapping local business and expertise to deliver projects. The HEP ESCO has had a particular focus on public buildings of local authorities. According to the World Bank's analysis, the HEP ESCO experience highlights several upsides and downsides. On the positive side, the HEP ESCO benefitted from the utility's corporate image and strong credit worthiness. It could also gain access to HEP's customer database. A major drawback, however, was the need to apply HEP's human resources and compensation policies, which were not well suited to the company's needs for experienced staff.
- India's Energy Efficiency Services Limited (EESL) was established in 2009 as a state-owned ESCO, a joint venture of four public enterprises under the Ministry of Power, to finance and

deliver energy efficiency solutions, especially in the residential and public sectors. In the residential sector, EESL designed and implemented the UJALA programme to make energy-efficient household lighting systems affordable for all. Using an original approach consisting in aggregating demand for and bulk procurement of appliances and equipment as well as providing innovative up-front payment options to consumers (e.g. on-bill financing), EESL managed to reduce the price of LEDs to USD 0.56 in 2017 down from USD 4.60 per bulb in 2014. This subsequently led to a similar decrease in the retail market (from USD 8.20 to USD 2.20) during the same period). As of January 2022, over 360 million LED bulbs have been distributed. Up to 80% price reduction in retail costs and up to 90% in procurement prices for LED bulbs have been achieved, along with improvement of technical specifications and boosting of the local manufacturing industry. In the public sector, EESL has run the Street Lighting National Program (SLNP), consisting in the roll-out of LEDs in public street lighting. Under the programme, the entire up-front investment for streetlights is made by EESL and recovered from the energy savings of municipalities over the project duration, using the deemed savings M&V approach. Using this approach notably helped demonstrate its viability as the basis for EPC used by private ESCOs. Similar to the UJALA programme, the procurement of large volumes from a variety of suppliers that meet strong technical standards also helped spur development of manufacturing capacity in India, lowering the price of energy efficiency measures. In total, over 6 million streetlights have been deployed so far.

- Saudi Arabia's National Energy Services Company (NESCO), also known as Tarshid, was created in 2017 by the Public Investment Fund with an initial capitalisation of over USD 500 million, to increase energy efficiency uptake by the public sector. This was complemented by a royal decree obligating all government bodies to exclusively contract with Tarshid. In turn, Tarshid has set up a framework for competitively procuring the services of private ESCOs through EPCs to deliver energy efficiency projects while also helping build local ESCO capacity. Equally, Tarshid has supported the development of transaction tools and EPC templates as well as guidelines for the measurement and verification of energy savings as per international benchmarks. This Super ESCO is intending to cover 70% of all projects in the country's energy efficiency sector, estimated to be an over USD 11 billion market.

Source: (World Bank, 2018[8]); (IEA, 2021[10])

Public-Private Partnership (PPP) models

Another potential option to procure (and finance) energy efficiency projects in the Philippines is through PPPs, which have been widely used globally to fund large infrastructure projects, such as airports, toll roads or power plants. PPPs are contracts entailing a long-term contractual agreement between the government and a private sector partner. The private party is often responsible for the design, construction, financing, operation, management and delivery of the service for a pre-determined period, receiving its compensation from fixed unitary payments (i.e. availability payment) or user-fees.

PPP models have been successfully implemented in the Philippines, with several airports, dam and toll road projects having been developed (OECD, 2016[11]) (PPP Centre, 2022[12]). This was greatly aided by a comprehensive legal framework for PPP, notably enshrined in the BOT Law passed in 1987. Notwithstanding, PPPs have been largely untapped in the renewable and energy efficiency sectors. This is explained by, first, the lack of familiarity with clean energy projects of LGUs as well as, in many cases, their limited experience in undertaking complex contractual arrangements (including evaluating solicited and unsolicited proposals). Equally, the fact that current PPP documents and procedures are still geared towards traditional, large-scale infrastructure projects makes it difficult to design PPP models adapted to the size and characteristics of energy efficiency projects. Still, while these issues are common globally, some countries have already developed PPP models for energy efficiency, with promising results. This is notably the case of Indonesia, which implemented a pilot project in Surakarta city (see Box 3.3).

To address these issues, there is a need to continue developing the capacity of LGUs, notably through targeted training activities for government officials (e.g. on the design of PPP programme, evaluation of project proposals and value for money, organisation of tenders from pre-selection through to monitoring of PPP implementation). Similarly, project development and transaction advisory could help government agencies and LGUs develop a pipeline of energy efficiency PPP projects. In this regard, the PPP centre (a government body dedicated to the promotion of PPP models in the country) has been active and providing training on PPPs, albeit not yet specifically on energy efficiency.

Training activities could draw from the experience of some LGUs, which are more advanced in developing their own sub-national PPPs. For instance, the Provincial Government of Albay, Bicol has notably been implementing ordinances for pursuing their PPP programme, offering a streamlined and simplified approval process that complies with national policy and guidance. The Mandanas-Garcia ruling by the Supreme Court in 2018, spearheaded by Batangas, which strengthens fiscal decentralisation among LGUs, was also raised in relation to sourcing funds for energy efficiency projects. At this point in time, this is the exception rather than the rule.

Box 3.3. Indonesia's Street Lighting PPP project in the municipality of Surakarta

The Surakarta's Street lighting project was initiated by the municipality of Surakarta on Java Island in 2018 in a bid to revamp and extend previous public street lighting infrastructure covering around 976 km (of which, 335 km of strategic roads). The project was undertaken following a 2016 survey showing both qualitative and quantitative shortcomings of previous public lighting infrastructure. On the one hand, the survey showed that numerous lamps and poles were non-compliant with national standards and that significant savings could be achieved through replacing lamp points with more energy-efficient LED lamps. On the other hand, the survey highlighted that previous lighting infrastructure did not satisfy actual needs estimated at around 31,890 lamp points (against 21,222 in 2016).

The project is being prepared under PPP arrangements (following presidential regulation 38/2015) with the municipality of Surakarta as the Government Contracting Agency. The municipality completed and submitted a final business case to prospective developers in mid-2020. Following a prequalification process held in end of 2020, three consortia of local and international companies are expected to bid for the 17-year concession. The winning bidder will be responsible for building, financing, operating and maintaining Surakarta's public street. The project's forecasted internal rate of return was estimated at 13.24% over 17 years, which is lower than rates observed for energy efficiency in Singapore and the Philippines, often in the upper teens. The project's indicative financial information is summarised in the table below.

Table 3.1. Surakarta's street lighting PPP project financials

Estimated project cost	Debt level	Equity level	Project IRR	Equity IRR
USD 25.7 million (17 years)	70%	30%	13.24%	15%

Note: IRR= Internal Rate of Return*. The internal rate of return is a financial metric used to estimate the profitability of potential investments. The internal rate of return is a discount rate that makes the net present value of all cash flows equal to zero in a discounted cash flow analysis.

The project will benefit from Ministry of Finance assistance under its Project Development Facility and is expected to reach financial close in late 2023. The project will also benefit from a government payment guarantee administered by the Indonesia Infrastructure Guarantee Fund to guarantee availability payment* by the Municipality.

Figure 3.2. Financing structure of the Surakarta public street lighting project

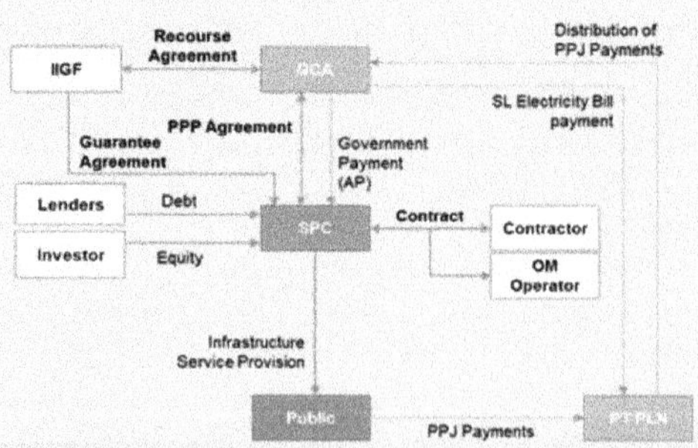

*AP=Availability Payments made by the public agency or institution based on particular project milestones, including a completion deadline and/or facility performance standards. GCA=Government Contracting Agency. OM= Operation and Maintenance. PPJ= Pajak Penerangan Jalan or Street Lighting Tax.SL= Street Lighting. SPC=Special Purpose Company.
Adapted from (OECD, 2021[13])

Furthermore, given the small size of energy efficiency projects, devising means to aggregate projects and implement them through PPPs is important to overcome this challenge. While a Super ESCO would be well placed to do that, there exists other potentially helpful conduits to achieve that, in the meantime. For instance, the provincial government could help co-ordinate and aggregate projects/buildings at the municipal/district level and structure them as PPPs. Economic zone authorities[3] or state universities, which cover areas with numerous public facilities, could also be well placed to identify and aggregate projects.

Financing options and development assistance for Philippine LGUs

Widening LGU's access to debt finance

In light of constraints regarding the government budget and the funding of energy efficiency projects entirely through cost recovery, tapping debt finance may be necessary to finance projects. Tightening public finances during the COVID crisis called for caution, however. In Q4 2022, the national government's (NG) debt reached a historically high level (PHP13.42 trillion) and stood at 60.9% of GDP according to the Bureau of Treasury. Fiscal deficit also widened from 3.4% in 2019 to 7.3% in 2022 (albeit down from a peak of 8.6% in 2021). Regardless, the country's debt burden remains relatively sustainable – e.g. external debt as a percentage of the GDP was recorded at 27.5% as of end-December 2022, while foreign currency reserves are at a sound level during the same period. Also, public finances are expected to improve as the economy recovers and returns to pre-pandemic levels.

At the subnational level, the situation is considerably different. LGUs' debt level amounted to less than 1% of GDP in 2022, despite the recent devolution of central government activities (Philstar, 2022[14]). Equally, only 62% of LGUs have borrowed money over the last five years while the Bureau of Local Government Finance estimated that LGUs utilise less than 50% of their borrowing capacity.

LGUs are yet to avail of credit to fund energy efficiency projects

LGUs are in theory allowed to access credit from commercial banks, whether public or private. However, in 2022, most outstanding loans were provided by state-owned banks (mainly from the Development Bank and the Land Bank of the Philippines). Prior to contracting a credit, LGUs must obtain a Certificate of Net Debt Coverage and Borrowing Capacity from the Department of Finance. Most notably, this document certifies that current debt service payment of LGUs do not exceed 20% of their annual regular income.

Credit facilities exist to support energy efficiency in public buildings. For instance, the Land Bank of the Philippines has put in place a special credit facility to fund energy efficiency-related expenditures for government entities (including LGUs). Still, few LGUs have availed of such credit facility, again pointing to a considerable lack of LGU awareness around energy efficiency and conservation opportunities.

Tapping the growing green bond market

The global green bond market has grown substantially over the last years. Taking advantage of this opportunity, the Philippines has issued several green bonds, the proceeds of which were, in part, used to fund energy projects. Still, most of the country's issuances came from the private sector, contrasting, for instance, with neighbouring Indonesia (another leading regional green bond issuer) whose green bonds were mostly issued at the sovereign level. Yet, green bond issuances could be a potential avenue to fund both central and local government's energy efficiency related investment, particularly as global investors scramble for green financial products. As the economy (and public finances conditions) recovers, this could be a potential financing avenue for the government to consider.

Municipal green bonds could also be an interesting source of financing for LGUs in the future, once LGUs are more at ease with bank lending and borrowing in general. Mexico City offers interesting insights into the potential for municipalities to tap the local or international green bond market. Indeed, the city is one of the very few municipalities of emerging economies to have issued a municipal green bond in 2017 to fund energy-efficient street lighting, railway transit as well as other sustainable sectors. The MXN 1-billion bond (with a five-year tenor) was rated triple A and was largely over-subscribed (Environmental Finance, 2017[15]).

Nevertheless, bond finance still represents a negligible share of total Philippine LGU borrowing (BLGF, 2022[16]). Hence, government has plans to foster LGU access to financial markets, notably through developing a municipal credit rating system to help build investors' confidence. As it does, it will also be important to concomitantly enhance LGUs' technical capacity to both raise funds in capital markets and bundle energy efficiency projects together (World Bank, 2018[2]).

Tapping public finance to mobilise private investment

Blended finance mechanisms including technical assistance can help support the financial structuring and enhance the risk profile of energy efficiency projects, notably through de-risking mechanisms. These could, for instance, take the form of first loss or non-payment guarantees as well as project preparation support to improve the capacity of project developers and financial institutions to access both domestic and international debt finance. Blended finance is typically administered by development finance institutions, whether domestic or international.

Based on stakeholder consultations, we showcase two potential blended finance instruments that were highlighted as having a high potential to mobilise private investment for energy efficiency in public building.

Energy efficiency funds

An energy efficiency revolving fund typically provides debt (and sometimes equity) financing to a government agency or private company to cover the investment cost of energy efficiency projects, which is then paid back from energy savings. Repayments (which often includes top-up charges in the form of interest or dividend payments) are then used to finance additional projects, thereby allowing the capital to "revolve". Energy efficiency revolving funds are typically capitalised using budget funds and/or international development finance. A key advantage of such funds is that they often offer lower rates than commercial bank loans while allowing a more efficient use of public money thanks to the fund's returns. In addition, the fund can be an effective way to demonstrate the viability of energy efficiency projects and help support market development.

Energy efficiency revolving funds have been used in several jurisdictions. This is notably the case of the energy efficiency and ESCO revolving funds in neighbouring Thailand. In particular, the ESCO revolving fund offers both access to a revolving credit line as well as equity financing to projects. The provision of equity funding is especially important to help facilitate ESCOs' access to finance and increase their borrowing capacity (see Box 3.4).

Box 3.4. Thailand's energy efficiency and ESCO revolving funds

Overview of Thailand's energy conservation funding mechanisms

In 1992, Thailand established its energy conservation (ENCON) fund to facilitate access to finance for energy efficiency and renewable energy projects. The fund mainly channels funding through three different mechanisms, namely: direct subsidies; the energy efficiency revolving fund; and the ESCO revolving fund. The fund's budget stems from a levy on petroleum products and, in 2017, had a total capital of USD 1.1 billion.

The fund's governance structure includes a committee, chaired by the Prime Minister and with members from various ministries, with decision-making authority and working-level sub-committees. The Ministry of Energy is responsible for monitoring and reporting on the performance of approved projects.

Figure 3.3. Thailand's energy conservation funding mechanism

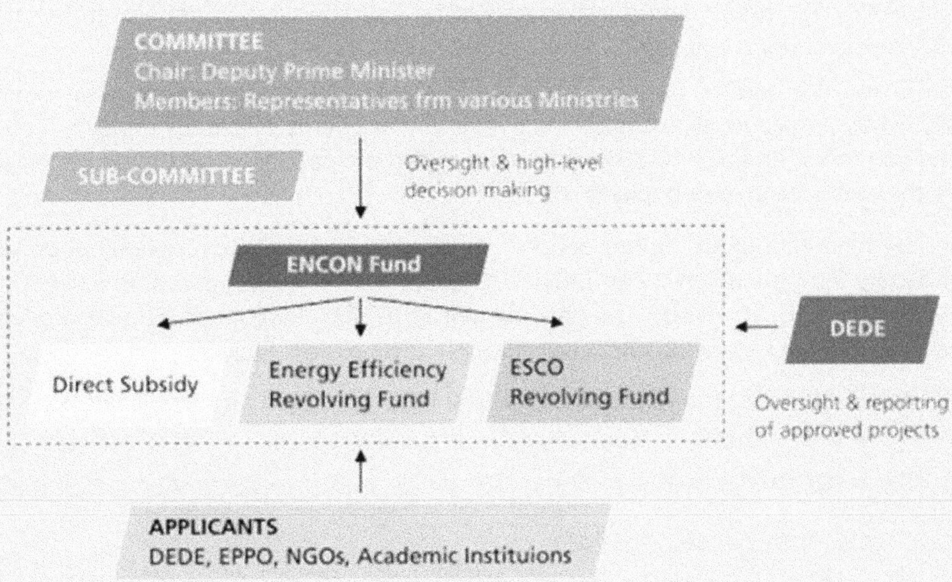

Source: Energy efficiency financing guidelines in Thailand: https://aqep.aseanenergy.org/wp-content/uploads/2019/05/EEF-Guideline-in-Thailand.pdf.

Direct subsidies

Direct subsidies can be provided to cover part of energy efficiency equipment costs. These can go to up to 20% (mainly for large industrial facilities), 30% for MSMEs, and 40% for unproven/new technologies. In any case, maximum funding amount per project is THB 6 million (or around current USD 165,000).

Energy efficiency revolving fund

The energy efficiency revolving fund was established in 2003 to help familiarise financial institutions with energy efficiency and renewable energy projects. The fund provides 0%-interest credit lines to financial institutions who then on-lend it to projects, which are assessed against a set of eligibility criteria. The fund was allocated in different phases. Phases 1-5 support 295 projects (60% of which were energy efficiency) for a total amount of USD 216 million. Phases 6 & 6+ supported around 160 projects as of 2019, mainly energy efficiency, and had a total budget of USD 126.3 million.

ESCO revolving fund

The ESCO revolving fund was established in 2008 to help mobilise investment in both energy efficiency and renewable energy projects while supporting the development of an ESCO market in Thailand. Unlike the energy efficiency revolving fund (managed by the ENCON fund), the ESCO revolving fund is managed by two independent fund managers with respective technical expertise in energy efficiency and renewable energy.

The ESCO fund can support projects through three mechanisms i.e.:

- **Project equity financing**, whose size can be as low as 10% to as high as 50% of the projects, with an absolute limit of USD 1.5 million. The ESCO revolving shall also not exceed the single majority shareholder. Investment period should be less than seven years with an exit price fixed at 4% share dividend cumulated and paid out upon exit.
- **Equipment leasing**, allow the leasing of equipment (up to 100% cost and no more than USD 600,000). Repayment duration should be less than five years and a flat interest rate of 3.5% per annuum is applied.
- **ESCO venture capital**, through which the ESCO revolving fund enters into a joint venture with ESCO companies to raise capital for investment in energy efficiency projects. In that case, the fund can take a stake of 10-30% max of the registered capital – investment period and exit price are the same for project equity financing.

In addition, the fund also offers further support services to ESCOs. Most notably, it operates a credit guarantee facility through which it can provide projects with a credit guarantee to support access to finance, limited to THB 10 million (roughly current USD 234 thousand). It also provides technical assistance to ESCOs in key areas (including through GHG project facility).

As of 2019, the ESCO revolving has invested a total USD 32 million and mobilised USD 155 million of investment in 145 EPC projects.

Source: ACE (2019), Energy efficiency financing guidelines in Thailand: https://agep.aseanenergy.org/wp-content/uploads/2019/05/EEF-Guideline-in-Thailand.pdf; Thailand's ESCO Revolving Fund's official webpage: http://www.efe.or.th/escofund.php?task=&sessid=&lang=en.

Risk-sharing facilities and energy saving insurance (ESI)

A risk-sharing facility can help overcome the high perceived risk of energy efficiency projects. Acting as a guarantee, such a facility can help backstop a variety of risks, particularly those related to credit risks or energy savings. Such a facility can help lower the cost of financing of LGUs and project proponents. It can take the form of, for instance, a partial credit guarantee or a first-loss mechanisms (wherein the guarantor absorbs losses until a certain maximum amount). India's Partial Credit Risk Sharing Facility for energy efficiency is a good example. This facility provides partial default risk coverage to 14 partner financial institutions on loans to energy efficiency projects implemented by 18 approved ESCOs via energy savings performance contracts; it also provides technical assistance and capacity building to ESCOs, which are key enabling factors in risk sharing facilities (OECD, 2022[17]). Thailand's credit guarantee facility (discussed in Box 3.4) under its ESCO revolving fund is another illustration.

In the same fashion, the ESI model is another option to help guarantee proceeds from energy savings through an insurance policy (usually covering a period sufficient to recover the investment). The ESI model was first pioneered by the Inter-American Development Bank (IDB) (IDB, 2020[18]) in Colombia and, due to its success, it is now being replicated in Brazil, Chile, Mexico and other Latin American countries, usually in co-operation with national development banks. The core components of an ESI model include a standardised EPC, an independent validation, the energy savings insurance and a financing structure or credit line, often structured under concessional terms. Newer projects have also integrated a digital monitoring platform. It is currently also piloted in a few select countries in Europe, as well as Morocco. While ESI schemes main focus so far has been on the MSME sector, such a model could potentially be adapted also for LGUs.

Figure 3.4. IDB's ESI model

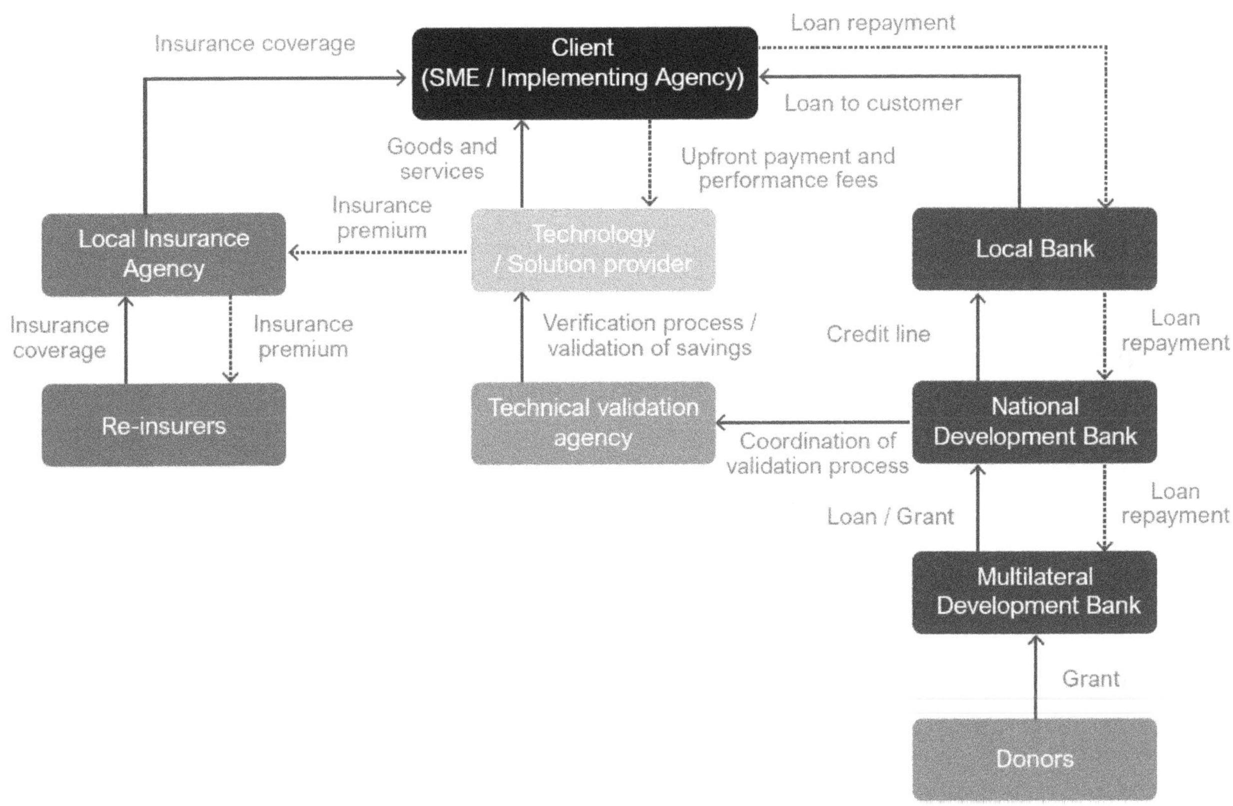

Source: (IDB, 2020[18])

Roadmap to 2030

The Government of the Philippines has been taking key actions to accelerate finance and investment in energy efficiency projects. A lot of efforts are underway to improve the energy efficiency of public buildings, benefiting from existing legislation (Republic Act No. 11285). These will be important to meet the country's clean energy goals as well as the objectives of the Paris Agreement. To support these efforts, this Roadmap highlights six recommendations to support the Philippines' efforts.

Recommendations

Enabling environment and tools

The updated National Energy Efficiency and Conservation Plan (NEECP) provides an opportunity to mainstream energy efficiency into LGU plans and activities.

i. The updated National Energy Efficiency Plan (NEECP) 2023 – 2050 provides an opportunity to reinforce targets, investment signals and mainstream energy efficiency into LGU plans and activities. Clear and time-bound sectoral targets can guide decision making and create a unified direction for energy efficiency investments in public buildings.

ii. Strengthened building energy codes, as well as voluntary or mandatory green building certification schemes, for new and existing construction, can ensure high energy efficiency standards for public buildings. This should include building envelopes, material efficiency and efficiency of end uses.

iii. In line with this, a strengthening and expansion of minimum energy performance standards for key appliances and equipment, together with energy technology lists (containing pre-assessed and pre-approved technologies complying with the desired efficiency standards) could be considered, and actively used in procurement processes.

iv. The Government can continue to encourage LGUs in mainstreaming energy efficiency within their plans and activities through information campaigns, guidelines issuance and targeted training (e.g. for energy efficiency and conservation officers). The latter can be developed in collaboration and assisted by international development partners. Support to adopt, regularly update and monitor progress towards the plan's objective will also be important.

v. The Government should also continue collecting data and information around government facilities' energy profile in order to ensure regular monitoring and target adequate actions (including for LGU's lagging behind).

Continue implementing capacity building and awareness raising programmes to support LGUs in availing of energy efficiency opportunities.

i. International development assistance could notably provide capacity building support for LGUs and financial institutions in key areas such as energy efficiency policies and savings potential for buildings, appliances and key end-use sectors. Other focus areas in need of capacity building are public procurement, origination and implementation of energy efficiency projects, access to capital markets, PPP for energy efficiency.

ii. The PPP centre could be an interesting conduit to help deliver training on PPP for energy efficiency, building on the country's experience in other infrastructure sectors. With support from international development partners, training and awareness campaigns can address different target groups ranging from policy makers/LGUs to technology providers and industry professionals, as well as financial institutions, commercial end-users and civil society.

Accommodate and expedite the procurement of energy efficiency projects – either through implementing specific carve-outs or rule change.

i. Recent regulation to allow the reuse of the proceeds of energy savings is a step in the right direction, albeit more is needed to encourage wide adoption of the scheme. In addition to information campaigns, other rules (e.g. limits to multi-year contracting or "mixed goods" procurement) could be usefully revisited to accommodate the procurement of energy efficiency projects through energy performance contracts.

ii. In this regard, the government-led implementation of demonstration projects within the facilities of selected LGUs/Government entities could go a long way to trial and evaluate the impact of any possible rule change as well as to prove concept, given the limited capacity of the Government / PNOC-RC to support energy efficiency improvements in public buildings.

iii. A specified number of LGUs are selected and funded on a competitive basis. For example, DOE may consider auctioning a predetermined amount to fund the pilot projects. The projects are selected on the merits of their proposals and judged by an independent panel of experts or advisers.

iv. As a fully funded project by the national government budget allocation, the procurement process could be simplified by exempting the pilot LGU from the requirements of Republic Act 9184, to allow LGUs to engage in mixed contracts such as EPCs. Given sufficient flexibility to experiment on feasible structures and approaches, the pilot scheme could provide valuable lessons that could inform subsequent adaptations for future projects.

v. The next round of pilot schemes could incorporate the lessons from the previous round. The DOE may choose to repeat this process, until experience, track record and technical competencies are built amongst the public and private sectors for broader applications to the covered LGUs and government buildings.

The Philippines can explore opportunities to strengthen the private ESCO market and encourage more private sector involvement in energy efficiency.

i. The Philippines has a favourable regulatory environment for promoting ESCO models (UNEPCCC, 2023[9]). Building on this and drawing from international lessons learned, the government can evaluate the possibility of establishing an aggregator entity for public energy efficiency projects amongst LGUs, similar to existing alternatives in the private sector. This can help with the creation of a pipeline of public sector projects that can be implemented through private sector ESCOs.

ii. Continuous capacity building measures, dedicated financing windows for ESCO projects, and potentially an Energy Savings Insurance (ESI) scheme adapted for public buildings, can also contribute to the creation of a more vibrant energy efficiency market.

Financing tools

Carefully evaluate opportunities to increase budget allocation to LGUs for energy efficiency, including private financing.

i. While sound public finances should remain a key priority, it will be important to ensure LGUs (particularly in less urbanised areas) have sufficient financial and human resources to comply with government requirements and targets. In particular, LGUs should be given enough resources to appoint an energy efficiency and conservation officer, or at least, mutualise that of nearby LGUs to lower transaction cost, when possible. This will be particularly important in the early stages of deployment of energy efficiency projects (to collect data, establish a baseline and identify opportunities) while continuing to diversify sources of funding over time (whether this be from concessional lending or directly from financial markets).

ii. The size of energy efficiency projects tends to fall below the thresholds of lending of private banks. For government entities, borrowing is limited to state-owned banks, where LandBank and the Development Bank of the Philippines are the two qualifying entities. For the initial pilot projects, the funding needed may be met with budgetary allocations.

Increase awareness on the availability of dedicated financing windows for energy efficiency projects. Implement a strategy to tap into these resources and diversify the funding available to LGUs and private ESCOs.

i. As few LGUs have yet used external sourcing of funding (either bonds or loans), international development partners can educate and support LGUs in designing a robust and realistic strategy to tap credit and capital markets, including to fund energy efficiency projects. This can be complemented with international and cross-government experience exchanges. In line with this, the early inclusion of third-party certification could be considered to attract investors and create confidence.

ii. Increased awareness on the available commercial funding and an open dialogue between lenders and energy efficiency project promoters can help LGUs understand the requirements and conditions of an economically viable project.

iii. The creation of an Energy Efficiency Revolving fund (drawing for instance from the Thai model) could help ESCOs and LGUs access long term concessional finance and/or equity and, in its early days, help support the deployment of demonstration projects. Such a fund, could for example, be capitalised from a "real property" tax (also known as Amilyar).

References

BLGF (2022), *LGU Credit Financing*, https://blgf.gov.ph/lguloans/. [16]

Business World Online (2022), “Energy dep’t touts savings from power conservation program”, *Energy dep’t touts savings from power conservation program*, https://www.bworldonline.com/economy/2022/12/27/495498/energy-dept-touts-savings-from-power-conservation-program/ (accessed on April 2023). [1]

DoE (2022), *List of ESCO Accredited Companies as of June 2022*, https://www.doe.gov.ph/energy-efficiency/list-esco-accredited-companies-june-2022. [6]

DoF / LCEP (2021), *The Philippine Sustainable Finance Roadmap*, https://www.dof.gov.ph/wp-content/uploads/2021/10/ALCEP-Roadmap.pdf. [7]

Efficiency, C. (2020), *Business models for energy efficiency - Energy Performance Contracting (presentation)*, https://c2e2.unepccc.org/wp-content/uploads/sites/3/2021/01/business-models-for-energy-efficiency-energy-performance-contracting.pdf. [5]

Environmental Finance (2017), *Bond of the year: Municipal - Mexico City*, https://www.environmental-finance.com/content/awards/green-bond-awards-2017/winners/bond-of-the-year-municipal-mexico-city.html. [15]

IDB (2020), *Energy Savings Insurance: Advances and Opportunities for Funding Small- and Medium-Sized Energy Efficiency and Distributed Generation Projects in Chile,*, https://publications.iadb.org/en/energy-savings-insurance-advances-and-opportunities-funding-small-and-medium-sized-energy. [18]

IEA (2021), *Evolving Energy Service Companies in China*. [10]

OECD (2022), *Clean Energy Finance and Investment Roadmap of India: Opportunities to Unlock Finance and Scale up Capital*, Green Finance and Investment, OECD Publishing, Paris, https://doi.org/10.1787/21b6e411-en. [17]

OECD (2022), *First OECD-DOE Workshop: Unlocking finance and investment for clean energy in the Philippines*. [3]

OECD (2021), *Clean Energy Finance and Investment Policy Review of Indonesia*, https://www.oecd-ilibrary.org/finance-and-investment/clean-energy-finance-and-investment-policy-review-of-indonesia_0007dd9d-en. [13]

OECD (2016), *OECD(2016), OVERVIEW OF THE PHILIPPINES’ PPP FRAMEWORK AND PROGRAMME Meeting of the South East Asia Regional Policy Network on PPP, Infrastructure and Connectivity*, https://one.oecd.org/document/GOV/PGC/SBO(2016)1/en/pdf. [11]

Philstar (2022), *DOF: LGU borrowing capacity still underutilized*, https://www.philstar.com/business/2022/11/25/2226207/dof-lgu-borrowing-capacity-still-underutilized. [14]

PPP Centre (2022), *List of PPP projects*, https://ppp.gov.ph/list-of-projects/. [12]

UNEPCCC (2023), *Regulatory Barriers for Energy Service Companies*. [9]

World Bank (2018), *The Philippines: Options for Financing Energy Efficiency in Public Buildings*, https://openknowledge.worldbank.org/handle/10986/29615. [2]

World Bank (2018), *Transforming Energy Efficiency Markets in Developing Countries: The Emerging Possibilities of Super ESCO*, https://openknowledge.worldbank.org/bitstream/handle/10986/30385/129781-BRI-PUBLIC-VC-ADD-SERIES-6-9-2018-12-9-31-LWLJfinalOKR.pdf?sequence=1&isAllowed=y. [8]

World Bank (2010), *Public Procurement of Energy Efficiency Services: Lessons from International Experience*,. [4]

Notes

[1] These cover: 158 public buildings for which the Department of Energy (DOE) had collected data as well as the walk-through audits of 20 buildings.

[2] According to the definition by the Government of the Philippines, this is classified as an "energy efficiency and conservation" measure.

[3] Economic Zone Authorities in the Philippines, promote and oversee established economic zones, which are intended to promote and attract foreign investments.

Annex A. Enabling policies and legal acts in the Philippines

Table A A.1. Enabling policies and legal acts for investors in the energy sector

Republic Act No. 9136	Also known as the Electric Power Industry Reform Act of 2001 (EPIRA). This promotes the utilization of indigenous, new and RE in power generation to reduce dependence on imported energy.
Republic Act No. 9513	Also known as the Renewable Act of 2008. This aims to accelerate the exploration, development, utilization, and commercialization of RE by institutionalizing the development of national and local capabilities in the use of RE systems and promoting its efficient and cost-effective commercial application by providing fiscal and non-fiscal incentives.
Executive Order No. 30	This creates the Energy Investment Coordinating Council to streamline regulatory procedures pertaining to energy projects.
Republic Act No. 11032	Also known as the Ease of Doing Business Act of 2018. This seeks to increase efficiency by reducing processing time, eliminating red tape, and curbing corrupt bureaucratic practices.
Republic Act No. 11234	Also known as the Energy Virtual One-Stop Shop (EVOSS) Act. This establishes a web-based monitoring system for energy applications and permits, which is shared by all agencies and entities involved in the approval process. EVOSS Implementing Rules and Regulations are outlined in Department Circular No. DC2019-05-0007.
Department Circular No. DC2019-10-0013	This lays down the Omnibus Guidelines governing the award and administration of RE, and the registration of RE Developers.
National Renewable Energy Program	Also known as NREP, it sets a target of at least 35% RE share in the country's power generation mix by 2030, and 50% by 2040.
Republic Act No. 11285	Also known as the Energy Efficiency and Conservation Act. It aims to institutionalize energy efficiency and conservation, enhance the efficient use of energy, and grant incentives to energy efficiency and conservation projects.
Renewable Portfolio Standards	Requires industry participants to source or produce a specified portion of their supply from eligible RE facilities. There is an increase in the minimum annual on-grid RE percentage increment from 1% to 2.52% starting 2023.
Net-Metering Programme	Allows end-users to generate electricity from RE-based systems up to 100 kW for own use and sell their excess to the grid.

Department Circular No. DC2021-11-0036	This lays down the Guidelines for the Green Energy Auction Program (GEAP), which intends to provide additional market for RE through a competitive electronic bidding of RE capacities. The first auction covered 2,000 MW in capacity.
Department Circular No. DC2021-05-0011	Establishes the guidelines, rules, and procedures in the endorsement of energy efficiency projects to the BOI for registration in order to grant fiscal incentives to the proponents for the said project.
IAEECC Resolution No. 5 s. 2022 or the Government Energy Management Programs (GEMP) Guidelines	Details the processes, procedures and additional guidelines for the implementation of the GEMP as mandated under the EE&C Act, and provide guidelines for the evaluation, approval, procurement, implementation and financing of Government Energy Efficiency Projects (GEEPs).
Department Circular No. DC2022-03-0004	Establishes the procedures and criteria for the evaluation, approval, and endorsement of the EE Strategic Investments covering New and Expansion of EE Projects to the BOI for the advantage of Fiscal Incentives.
Department Circular No. DC2022-11-0034	Prescribing Amendments to Section 19 Of Department Circular No. DC2009-05-0008 Titled, Rules and Regulations Implementing Republic Act No. 9513, Otherwise Known as "The Renewable Energy Act of 2008" (Easing foreign ownership limitation)
Department Circular No. DC2023-05-0009	This prescribed the GEMP Guidelines on Strengthening the EEC Professionals, adoption of Training Modules for Capacity Building and providing for Certification Process for the Recognition of Training Institution.

Table A A.2. Energy efficiency guidelines and resolutions issued by the Inter-Agency for Efficiency and Conservation Committee Resolutions

IAEECC Resolution No. 1 s. 2020	Directs all government entities to comply with the GEMP, orders the DOE to conduct energy audits and spot checks, and submit proposed improvements to the GEMP
IAEECC Resolution No. 2 s. 2021	Directs all government entities to use energy efficient light emitting diode (led) lamps in government buildings and facilities as a requirement for compliance to GEMP
IAEECC Resolution No. 3 s. 2021	Directs all government entities to use inverter type air-conditioning units or similar technologies in government buildings and facilities as a requirement for compliance to the GEMP
IAEECC Resolution No. 4 s. 2021	Enjoins the Council of Good Local Governance to consider, include and adopt the EEC as one of the areas in the criteria per Section 7 of Republic Act No. 11292 - "The Seal of Good Local Governance Act of 2019"
IAEECC Resolution No. 5 s. 2022	Directs all government entities to observe the approved GEMP Guidelines
IAEECC Resolution No. 6 s. 2022	Recommends to the Governance Commission for Government-Owned or -Controlled Corporation (GCG) to consider, include, and adopt EEC as one criterion in the performance evaluation system for Government-Owned or -Controlled Corporations (GOCCs) in the grant of performance-based incentives
IAEECC Resolution No. 7 s. 2023	Encouraging the adoption of flexible work arrangements for all government entities as part of the government's EEC Measures under the GEMP

www.ingramcontent.com/pod-product-compliance
Ingram Content Group UK Ltd.
Pitfield, Milton Keynes, MK11 3LW, UK
UKHW051507290926
15471UKWH00008B/1471

9 789264 977426